Gaston 1/81 £6-95 22 Sept

D1356074

Poets' London

Longman Travellers Series

Poets' London

PADDY KITCHEN
Line drawings by Wendy Dowson

Longman *London and New York*

Dedication

To Colleen and Charles Stuart-Jervis

Longman Group Limited London

*Associated companies, branches and representatives
throughout the world*

© Paddy Kitchen 1980

First published 1980

British Library Cataloguing in Publication Data

Kitchen, Paddy
  Poets' London. – (Longman travellers series).
  1. Poets, English – Homes and haunts – England
  – London metropolitan area   2. London –
  Description – 1951- – Guide-books
  I. Title
  914.21′04′857   DA689.L7   79-42871

  ISBN 0-582-50283-7

Set in 10/12pt V-I-P Palatino
Printed in Great Britain by
William Clowes (Beccles) Ltd, Beccles and London

Contents

Acknowledgements

We are grateful to the following for permission to reprint and publish copyright material:

Sir John Betjeman and John Murray (Publishers) Ltd for extracts from *Monody on the Death of Aldersgate Street Station*, *The Metropolitan Railway*, and *Middlesex*; the Estate of the late Richard Church for extracts from *Hay's Wharf* by Richard Church; the Executors of the W. H. Davies Estate for extract from *An Old House in London* by W. H. Davies; the Literary Trustees of Walter de la Mare and The Society of Authors as their representative for *A Young Girl* and extract from *Fare Well* by Walter de la Mare; Maureen Duffy for extract from *Taking Down the Runners* published in *Memorials of the Quick & the Dead* (Hamish Hamilton Ltd); Faber and Faber Ltd for extracts from *Four Quartets*, *The Waste Land*, and *Preludes*, published in *Collected Poems 1909–1962* by T. S. Eliot; the Macmillan Company of London and Basingstoke and the National Trust for extracts from '*Mary, Pity Women*' and *The River's Tale* by Rudyard Kipling; Faber and Faber Ltd for extract from *Autumn Sequel* published in *The Collected Poems of Louis MacNeice*; David Higham Associates Ltd for extract from *Still Falls the Rain* published in *Collected Poems* by Edith Sitwell; the Executor, James MacGribbon for the poem *How do you see?* by Stevie Smith from *The Collected Poems of Stevie Smith*; Anthony Thwaite for extract from *On consulting 'Contemporary Poets of the English Language'* published in *A Portion for Foxes* (Oxford University Press).

The sources of the photographs used in this book are given at the end of their captions.

Introduction

Initially I set out to achieve in this guide a form which would combine thoroughness with shining clarity. As a kind of image of this ambition I repeated to myself Philip Larkin's lines from *The Whitsun Weddings*:

I thought of London spread out in the sun,
Its postal districts packed like squares of wheat . . .

But things didn't work out quite like that – apart from anything else, most of the outdoor research was done during an exceptionally cold, wet winter.

Tracing the paths of poets tends to leave on the mind an impression rather like the random trails of a Jackson Pollock painting; and the layout of London itself is not easy to divide into tidy quadrilaterals. Also it is difficult – well, impossible – to attempt to write a readable narrative and to be comprehensive. So I have not tried to squeeze in every recorded address associated with a poet, nor have I covered the complete London area. The main basis of the structure is, inevitably, geographical, and for the first eight chapters there is also an element of chronological development. Thus Chaucer features in the first chapter, *Westminster*; Shakespeare in the second, *Southwark*; Donne and Milton in the third, *The City*; Dryden and Pope in the fourth, *Covent Garden*; Blake in the fifth, *Strand, Fleet Street, Inns of Court and Holborn*; Keats and Coleridge in the sixth, *Hampstead and Highgate*; and Yeats and Eliot in the seventh, *Bloomsbury*. With the eighth chapter, *The West End*, the chronological element still persists with the presence of Dylan Thomas, but Lord Byron, by managing to confine his lodgings, love affairs, publisher and funeral procession to the West End, does tend to dominate. Alongside this vein of historical development cluster references in each chapter to poets from all ages, and many poets are referred to in several places. When a poet is mentioned for the first time, his or her dates are given, and also on subsequent occasions when it is felt this might be useful. Anyone wishing to find all the mentions of a specific poet will be able to do so by using the index at the end. And just before the index there is an appendix giving an alphabetical list of the 150 or so poets included in the text, together with their dates, occupations, and the titles of a brief selection of their works. Chapters 9 and 10, *The River* and *Margents*, include, respectively, information about very scattered sites along the Thames (from Deptford to Twickenham), and a selection of places in the environs of London. The final chapter, *Poetry now*, gives addresses and general advice concerning poetry readings, writing classes, libraries and bookshops.

Readers should perhaps be warned that not all the quotations included in the text were selected for their literary merit – in some cases topicality and curiosity outweigh elegance or depth. But there are also lyrics and extracts that represent some of the best of English poetry; a number are very familiar, others less so.

I was particularly glad that the publishers wanted to include original illustrations as well as photographs and reproductions, and delighted that they invited Wendy Dowson to do them. Her realization of the subjects which I suggested (without properly considering the problems I was posing for her) are remarkable for their imaginative response, and above all for their strength and accuracy in depicting London's architecture.

I should like to thank two members of my family for their practical participation in preparing this guide. My sister, Colleen Stuart-Jervis provided initial, and invaluable, area and author breakdowns of references from many sources. And my mother typed the final manuscript: eighty seems to be an excellent age for accuracy. (Any mistakes or misconceptions in the text are mine.) When my nephew, Roly, heard about the book, he wrote a poem called *Contaminated London* to remind us that the past wasn't all champagne and roses, and warning us not to over-romanticize. By allowing the poets to speak quite frequently for themselves, I hope I have avoided any cover-up of harsh practical realities, while at the same time giving enough space to the imaginative vision with which poetry has always illuminated the more intangible aspects of our lives. Certainly while preparing the book I was frequently aware of the weight of life that lies behind some of my brief references: of the poverty, the thwarted ambitions, the unrequited loves and premature deaths, as well as of the disciplined work, historical meetings, fulfilled passions, and rip-roaring good times. I hope I haven't sold too far short the poets who underwent these experiences by cramming them into a guide, but rather that they will each, however briefly, enhance the experience of visitors who are attracted to the world of poets' London.

Westminster Bridge and the Houses of Parliament.

CHAPTER 1

Westminster

When William Wordsworth crossed Westminster Bridge in the Dover coach at dawn on 3 September 1802, he witnessed a scene which inspired the sonnet that begins: 'Earth has not anything to show more fair'. The sun glittering on the 'Ships, towers, domes, theatres, and temples' was more beautiful than the first dawn of the world could have been, and he had never seen

> . . . never felt, a calm so deep!
> The river glideth at his own sweet will:
> Dear God! the very houses seem asleep;
> And all that mighty heart is lying still!

That particular bridge is now demolished, and if you stand on its replacement at dusk, when the office workers are beginning to stream home, the traffic is swerving and snarling along the wide road, and the helicopters with flashing lights are chuntering

overhead, it would be easy to assume that the deep calm which Wordsworth felt has been destroyed for ever. But it would also be wrong to assume that noise and stress are modern phenomena: right from medieval times there have been crowded, dirty corners in the city; and the satire and despair that may be found in some modern urban verse were present in even stronger forms 300 years ago. The lyrical or stately moods of some poetry may be more hard to rediscover in present-day London, but if one leaves the most popular sites, or eschews the conventional hours, it is not impossible.

Westminster Bridge at dawn is still much quieter than it is at dusk. The light along the river is the same which inspired Turner, Monet and Whistler; and the fires and factories will not pollute it later in the day as they did in Wordsworth's time, since central London is now by law a smokeless zone. As the traffic builds up, however, it certainly becomes a very noisy place; yet the sweep of the great grey river, the bass boom of Big Ben, and the solidity of the Greater London Council's offices on the south side, and Pugin and Barry's fervently gothic Houses of Parliament on the north, give a sense of permanence and power which overrides the ephemeral din of each taxi, lorry, car, motorbike and bus.

Poets' London begins here, straddling the Thames and remarking the anonymous visitors who have scribbled and scratched their names on the balustrade of the bridge, partly because Wordsworth's poem is perhaps the most famous London poem of all, and partly because Poets' Corner in Westminster Abbey is close at hand. Like attending a crowded party where famous guests are expected and introductions hard to catch above the hubbub, a visit to Poets' Corner will provide cues for an abbreviated sampling of English poets. It also provides a convenient opportunity to begin more or less at the beginning with Geoffrey Chaucer (*c.* 1343–1400), whose scarred gothic memorial tomb lies in the Abbey.

In the fourteenth century Westminster and London were two distinct and separate cities, with plenty of grass and trees and views of the river, and both were well known to Chaucer, who was a court poet and also held several offices in the king's household. One of these was a two-year appointment under Richard II as Clerk of the King's Works when he was responsible, among other things, for the maintenance and repair of the Palace of Westminster, which stood where the Houses of Parliament are now, and was the chief royal residence. During that time he would have known Henry Yevele, who partially designed the nave of the Abbey which was then being rebuilt, and who was the King's Master Mason. Chaucer's wife was a sister of John of Gaunt's third wife, and Gaunt was for a long time Chaucer's patron and protector. When Gaunt's son, Henry IV, secured Richard II's abdication in 1399, he increased Chaucer's annuity and confirmed the yearly grant of a tun of wine which Richard had recently made. A few years earlier he had given Chaucer the fur to embellish a floor-length scarlet gown as a singular mark of respect for his talents. In the year of Henry's accession, Chaucer took a lease on a house in the garden of the chapel of St Mary, Westminster, next door to the 'White Rose Tavern'. (These buildings were later destroyed to make room for Henry VII's Chapel at the east end of the Abbey.) It was in this house that he spent the last year of his life, and rounded off *The Canterbury Tales* on which he had been working for twelve years. The original design had included some 120 tales, but this was too ambitious and only twenty-four were written. Despite royal patronage, however, Chaucer's finances were sometimes shaky, and some of the last poems he wrote were comic begging ones, including one to the king in which he likened the lightness of his purse to the fickleness of a lady.

A contemporary and friend of Chaucer's was the poet John Gower (*c*. 1330–1408), who during his lifetime was highly regarded and also enjoyed the patronage of Richard II. It is said that once when he was rowing on the Thames he met the royal barge, and the king invited him to audience and bade him write 'some new thing'. The result was *Confessio Amantis* – 34,000 rhymed couplets which he dedicated to the king and in which he complimented Chaucer. When Chaucer went abroad on diplomatic service, he nominated Gower as one of his attorneys, and at the end of *Troylus and Cryseyde* he wrote: 'O moral Gower, this book I directe / To thee'.

For many people, one of the most enduring images of this period is contained in the deathbed scene Shakespeare wrote for John of Gaunt in *Richard II* in which he praises England:

> This royal throne of kings, this scept'red isle,
> This earth of majesty, this seat of Mars,
> This other Eden, demi-paradise,
> This fortress built by Nature for herself
> Against infection and the hand of war . . .

3

And from contemporary paintings it would appear that the artists of the time found London and Westminster clean and bright and romantic.

Chaucer was buried in the Abbey at the entrance of St Benedict's chapel (where Dryden's monument is now), and at first his only memorial was a leaden plate hung on the adjacent pillar. Then in 1556 the minor poet Nicholas Brigham erected the present tomb – which was probably taken out of a dissolved monastery. A word of warning to newcomers to Westminster Abbey: it does get an enormous number of visitors, and steps have had to be taken to direct the flow of people, using at one point a built-up walkway. There is also an entrance fee to get beyond the nave to the part containing the chapels and Poets' Corner.

Geoffrey Chaucer and Westminster as it looked before its restoration by Wren.

Since the Reformation, the Abbey has been a place of burial and commemoration for some of the most famous and illustrious people in the land – and others whose reputations have since dimmed. The clustering and crowding of memorials and monuments make parts of the interior look rather like an overcrowded sculpture museum. As long as 200 years ago, Sir Joshua Reynolds commented that 'Westminster is already so stuffed with statuary it would be a deadly sin against taste to increase the squeeze of tombs there'. In her novel *Capital*, Maureen Duffy (b. 1933: also a poet and dramatist) describes a scene in which a character imagines that the marble and stone figures are 'poised as if frozen by an uplifted baton. Any moment it would fall and statesmen, generals, and admirals would waltz away up the nave.'

Poets' Corner is neither a corner nor confined to poets. It began as a corner, but then spread throughout the south transept, and it includes memorials to many kinds of writers, as well as people from other professions. A former poet laureate, Cecil Day Lewis (1904–72) remarked:

> It is, one might say, typical of the British way of life, not only in its apparent muddle, but in our tradition that writers should rub shoulders with men eminent in other fields. . . . The arbitrary and unplanned nature of the place is one of its most rewarding features: moralists may draw from it useful lessons about the transience of human reputations and the permanence of human values.

As one enters from the east, a memorial to John Dryden (1631–1700) stands in the middle of the bay at the west end of St Benedict's Chapel. Under the patronage of James II he had been poet laureate, but the revolution of 1688 deprived him of this post and he died in Soho in somewhat straitened circumstances. After argument, it was decided that he should be buried in the Abbey and his 'friends filled fifty carriages, and fifty more followed'. One observer remarked that the ceremony was both 'incongruous and burlesque'. At first the grave was unmarked, and then the Duke of Buckingham, prompted by Pope's allusion to Dryden's 'rude and nameless stone' erected a monument, and eleven years later the Duke's widow replaced an inferior bust with the present one by Peter Scheemakers, who designed many Abbey memorials.

The bust of Henry Wadsworth Longfellow (1807–82) was erected by his English admirers in 1884. He was a highly suitable poet for declaiming out loud in Victorian drawing-rooms – or even perhaps under one's breath as one looks at the memorials:

> Lives of great men all remind us
>   We can make our lives sublime,
> And, departing, leave behind us
>   Footprints on the sands of time.

Next is a monument to Abraham Cowley (1618–67) which claims he was the 'Pindar, Horace and Virgil of England', and he was certainly revered by both Milton and Dryden; but seventy years after his death Pope asked 'Who now reads Cowley?', which shows how quickly literary reputations can fade.

Chaucer's canopied tomb, to which the tradition of Poets' Corner owes its origin, looks very ancient and scarred amid so much polished marble; but it is a suitably unpretentious, yet solid edifice to the humane poet of whom Dryden said: 'Here is God's plenty'. Next to it is a memorial to John Philips (1676–1709) whose claim to fame is his poem *Cyder* in praise of the qualities of the apple; unfortunately these qualities did not prevent his dying of consumption at the age of thirty-three.

On the floor of the transept near by is set a cluster of stones commemorating Tennyson, Browning, Hopkins, Masefield, Eliot and Auden. Henry James's memorial is also there, and it would seem churlish not to mention it merely because he was a novelist rather than a poet; he in fact wrote an essay about Browning's burial in the Abbey, praising him above all 'on account of the extraordinary beauty of his treatment of the special relationship between man and woman'. Robert Browning (1812–89) died in Venice, twenty-eight years after the death of his wife Elizabeth Barrett Browning, and his body was brought to the Abbey and marked with a stone of Italian marbles and porphyry. His last work, *Asolando*, was published the day he died. Next to Browning lies Alfred, Lord Tennyson (1809–92), who became poet laureate in 1850. His poem *Crossing the Bar* was set to music and sung for the first time at his funeral; it ends:

> For tho' from out our bourne of Time and Place
> The flood may bear me far,
> I hope to see my Pilot face to face
> When I have crost the bar.

Three years later a commemorative bust was erected near by; it is by Thomas Woolner, one of the pre-Raphaelites.

Thomas Stearns Eliot (1888–1965) was buried in East Coker, Somerset, and in 1967 his memorial stone was placed in the Abbey. *East Coker*, the second of the *Four Quartets*, contains a most accurate and despairing description of the act of writing:

> So here I am, in the middle way, having had twenty years –
> Twenty years largely wasted, the years of *l'entre deux guerres* –
> Trying to learn to use words, and every attempt
> Is a wholly new start, and a different kind of failure

Because one has only learnt to get the better of words
For the thing one no longer has to say, or the way in which
One is no longer disposed to say it. And so each venture
Is a new beginning, a raid on the inarticulate . . .

The stone which covers the ashes of John Masefield (1878–1967),
poet laureate from 1930, commemorates a more optimistic
temperament, author of the popular *Sea Fever*:

I must down to the seas again, to the lonely sea and the sky,
And all I ask is a tall ship and a star to steer her by . . .

Above it is the memorial stone to Wystan Hugh Auden (1907–73),
installed in 1974; he was buried at Kirchstetten, Lower Austria.
And next to these is the memorial stone to Gerard Manley
Hopkins (1844–89), laid in 1975 on the centenary of the shipwreck
which inspired his great poem *The Wreck of the Deutschland*.
Hopkins, a Jesuit priest, was buried in Glasnevin, Dublin, and
would have been amazed to know that eighty-six years after his
death his memorial stone would touch the top of Tennyson's in
Westminster Abbey, his reputation having so increased during
the twentieth century.

Although, unlike Hopkins, George Gordon, Lord Byron
(1788–1824) was famous during his lifetime, it was not until 1969
that his white marble memorial tablet was installed. The reason
for this, the official guide to the Abbey tells us, was that 'for many
years the open profligacy of his life proved an obstacle to his
commemoration'; however, as the guide continues, 'his poetic
genius and mastery of the art of letter-writing at length
prevailed'. He died of fever in Missolonghi where he had gone to
join the Greek insurgents in their war of independence. A few
weeks before his death he wrote:

If thou regrett'st thy youth, *why live*?
  The land of honourable death
Is here: – up to the field, and give
    Away thy breath!

Seek out – less often sought than found –
  A soldier's grave, for thee the best;
Then look around, and choose thy ground,
    And take thy rest.

He is buried in the Byron family vault at Hucknall Torkard, Nottinghamshire. Matthew Arnold (1822–88) subdued his early romanticism, which was deeply influenced by Byron, to become an inspector of schools and thus caused no impediment to the erection of a memorial bust quite quickly after his death. It is on the window-sill above Poets' Corner door, and was presented by relatives and friends in 1891. Beside the door is a memorial to Michael Drayton (1563–1631), who was buried elsewhere in the Abbey; it carries lines by the poet Francis Quarles (1592–1644). On the night before he died, Drayton wrote some tender love verses ending:

> Soe all my Thoughts are peyces but of you
> Whiche put together makes a Glass soe true
> As I therin noe others face but yours can Veiwe.

On the floor near by a memorial tablet reminds us that 700 years before Chaucer, according to the historian Bede (673–735), an unlearned herdsman called Caedmon (active 670) suddenly received the power of song and entered a monastery and wrote scriptural verse.

Outside Poets' Corner door a tablet was placed in 1954 to commemorate the fact that William Caxton (*c*. 1424–91) set up the first printing press in England in a chapel very near that spot. He was buried somewhere on the site where St Margaret's Church now stands. The establishment of the first press in a chapel led to the word 'chapel' being used to describe any printing office or association of print workers and it is now applied to groups of members of trade unions in the printing industry.

Over a small doorway in the adjacent east wall is a memorial to Ben Jonson (1572–1637), which was erected about 100 years after Jonson's death. His grave is in the third bay of the north aisle of the nave and he is said to have been buried upright having told the Dean 'six feet long by two feet wide is too much for me. Two feet by two is all I want.' The original stone was removed in 1821 and placed against the nave wall and another put in its place. Both the memorial and the stones carry the inscription 'O rare Ben Johnson' – with a superfluous 'h'. Jonson died in a house which then stood between the Abbey and St Margaret's, paralysed and in debt (despite being poet laureate and having had much success as a dramatist and writer of masques for the court), but still full of his powers as a poet. As he wrote of himself:

. . . though thy Nerves be shrunke, and blood be cold
. . . curious fooles, and envious of thy straine,
May blushing sweare, no Palsi's in thy braine.

Samuel Butler (1612–80) – not to be confused with the nineteenth-century prose writer of the same name – whose memorial was erected next to Jonson's in 1721, was buried in St Paul's, Covent Garden, because there was no money to pay the Abbey fees for a burial. Author of *Hudibras*, which satirised the Puritans and delighted Charles II, he did not manage to retain popularity and patronage – the fate of many honest sceptics. His memorial was erected by John Barber, a printer and Lord Mayor, in order 'That he who had been denied almost everything in life might not in death be denied a tomb.'

Below the bust of Butler is a memorial to Edmund Spenser (*c*. 1552–99), author of *The Faerie Queene* which he dedicated to Queen Elizabeth. He died in a now demolished street near the Abbey, having fled from Ireland where his castle was burnt down in a sudden insurrection. His funeral is supposed to have been attended by Jonson, Beaumont, Fletcher, and possibly Shakespeare, all of whom wrote mournful elegies which they threw into the grave together with the pens that they had used. The memorial is a copy made in 1778 of one erected by the Countess of Dorset in 1620 which fell into disrepair. The exact site of Spenser's grave was not marked, but in 1938, at the instigation of the Bacon Society, the nearest grave to his memorial was excavated in the hope of finding the pens and elegies and evidence concerning the authorship of Shakespeare's plays (believed by some to have been written by Francis Bacon). A collapsed lead coffin was found, surrounded by dry powdery soil, but there was no trace of pen or parchment.

The monument to John Milton (1608–74), was not erected until sixty-three years after his death because of the strength of royalist feeling against his puritan views. Its installation was organised by William Benson, one of the king's auditors – who recorded this fact at some length on the memorial itself and caused Dr Johnson to remark to Boswell: 'Mr Benson has bestowed more words upon himself than upon Milton.' The memorial was sculpted by J. M. Rysbrack who designed many Abbey memorials, including the highly elaborate one to Isaac Newton in the nave. Milton was buried in St Giles, Cripplegate. The memorial that was designed to fit against the bottom of Milton's is to Thomas Gray (1716–71), who was buried at Stoke Poges, the scene of his *Elegy written in a Country Churchyard*. It portrays the lyric muse, who sits pointing up to Milton's bust with one hand while holding a medallion portrait of Gray in the other.

Bedecked with a laurel wreath, Thomas Shadwell (*c*. 1642–92) is framed by sculpted curtains, draped and tasselled. He superseded Dryden as poet laureate when William III became king after the 'Glorious Revolution'. He and Dryden were open rivals, Dryden having attacked Shadwell in his satire *MacFlecknoe*, which contains the following lines:

> The rest to some faint meaning make pretence,
> But Shadwell never deviates into sense.
> Some beams of wit on other souls may fall,
> Strike through and make a lucid interval;
> But Shadwell's genuine night admits no ray,
> His rising fogs prevail upon the day.

Shadwell died of opium poisoning in Chelsea, where he was buried. The extremely elaborate monument to Matthew Prior (1664–1721) is an indication of his contemporary reputation. He held several offices under William III, and was Plenipotentiary at the Court of Louis XIV. Louis provided the bust of Prior by Antoine Coysevox for the memorial, and the headmaster of Westminster School wrote the Latin epitaph. Prior had composed his own, innocuous, epitaph, but the Dean would not allow it to be used:

> To me 'tis given to dye, to you 'tis given
> To live; Alas! one moment sets us even.
> Mark how impartial is the will of Heaven!

A bust of Adam Lindsay Gordon (1833–70) by Lady Kennet stands on a column near Woolner's head of Tennyson. Gordon spent his adult life in Australia and wrote ballads about life in the bush. His memorial was unveiled by the Duke of York in 1934. The full-length figure of Thomas Campbell (1777–1844) stands on a pedestal inscribed with a rather long, if reasonably appropriate, quotation from his poem *Last Man*. He helped to found London University and regarded that as 'the only important event in his life's little history'. He died in Boulogne and was buried in the Abbey eighteen days later. High up on the right of Campbell's statue is a bust of Samuel Taylor Coleridge (1772–1834) by Hamo Thornycroft, which was donated by Dr Mercer, an American, in 1885 and unveiled by the Minister of the United States in London, James Russell Lowell. In his oration Lowell described Coleridge's poem *The Ancient Mariner* as 'marvellous in its mastery over delightfully fortuitous inconsequence that is the adamantine logic of dreamland'. Coleridge died and was buried in Highgate. His friend William Wordsworth (1770–1850), who was poet laureate, is commemorated with a statue by Frederick Thrupp showing the poet seated, his head slightly drooping in a characteristically thoughtful posture. Thomas Carlyle once described him as 'a man of immense head and great jaws like a crocodile's, cast in a mould designed for prodigious work'. He was buried at Grasmere in the Lake District.

Dr Samuel Johnson (1709–84), who was a poet as well as a lexicographer and critic, was buried in the Abbey near the grave of his pupil and friend, the actor David Garrick. His bust on the wall behind Wordsworth was made by Joseph Nollekens during Johnson's lifetime, and donated anonymously to the Abbey in 1939. Johnson did not like the way Nollekens had depicted him with so much hair, evidently in order to make him look more like 'an ancient poet', the hair being modelled 'from the flowing locks of a sturdy Irish beggar'. Above Johnson there is a bust of Robert Southey (1774–1843), who was poet laureate before his friend Wordsworth, and a brother-in-law of Coleridge. He rather neatly summed up his method in his poem *The Holy Tree*:

> I love to view these things with curious eyes,
>   And moralize . . .

The memorial to William Shakespeare (1564–1616) was the first to be erected in London – in 1740. It was organized by a group which included Alexander Pope, and partially paid for by benefit performances of Shakespeare plays at Drury Lane and Covent Garden. The design was by William Kent, and the work carried out by Scheemakers. The monument caused much criticism: one author claimed that 'the chief difficulty lies in the figure of Shakespeare himself – he leans upon a pedestal like a sort of sentimental fop', while Hugh Walpole called the whole thing 'preposterous', particularly the inclusion of the heads of Elizabeth I, Richard III and Henry V placed at angles at the base of the pedestal. The scroll which Shakespeare touches misquotes

Poets' Corner, Westminster Abbey. The large central memorial is Shakespeare's; others, from left to right, commemorate: Thomas Campbell (standing figure), S. T. Coleridge (bust), William Wordsworth (seated figure), Dr Johnson, Robert Southey, John Keats and P. B. Shelley (linked medallions), Robert Burns, James Thomson, and the three Brontë sisters, whose joint plaque is bottom right. (*Woodmansterne Ltd*)

Prospero's lines from *The Tempest* beginning: 'The cloud-capp'd towers, the gorgeous palaces'. Shortly after Shakespeare's death an unsuccessful bid was made to move his body from Stratford-upon-Avon to the Abbey. Ben Jonson referred to this in his *To the Memory of My Beloved, the Author Mr William Shakespeare*:

> Soul of the Age!
> The applause! delight! the wonder of our stage!
> My Shakespeare, rise; I will not lodge thee by
> Chaucer, or Spenser, or bid Beaumont lie
> A little further, to make thee a room:
> Thou art a monument, without a tomb,
> And art alive still, while thy book doth live,
> And we have wits to read, and praise to give.

Linked by a garland, two simple tablets commemorating John Keats (1795–1821) and Percy Bysshe Shelley (1792–1822) are on the wall above Shakespeare's memorial. They were erected by the Keats-Shelley Memorial Association in 1954 – Shelley's atheism having long prevented his commemoration in the Abbey. He drowned in the Gulf of La Spezia, and after a grisly cremation on the beach his ashes were taken to Rome and finally buried there after remaining for several months in the British Consul's wine cellar. Keats had died from consumption in Rome the year before, and Shelley attempted a very ambitious poem, *Adonais*, as a lament for the young poet he had considered would 'far surpass me'. Keats was able to obey his own dictum that poetry

> should strike the reader as a wording of his own highest thoughts, and appear almost a remembrance. Its touches of beauty should never be half-way, thereby making the reader breathless, instead of content. The rise, the progress, the setting of imagery should, like the sun, come natural to him.

The bust of Robert Burns (1759–96) was erected in 1885 and paid for in shilling subscriptions by his fellow Scots. Combining a passion for wine and women with a great talent for song, Burns is the only British poet who is also a popular hero. In Scotland the 25th of January is called Burns Night and celebrated with the proverbial flowing bowl. Many of Burns's poems are best known as songs, such as:

> O my Luve's like a red red rose
>   That's newly sprung in June:
> O my Luve's like the melodie
>   That's sweetly play'd in tune.

James Thomson (1700–48), whose memorial stands below Burns's and who was also a Scot, made his reputation with his four-part work *The Seasons*. His monument was designed by the great architect Robert Adam and erected in 1762.

Charlotte (1816–55), Emily (1818–48) and Anne (1820–49) Brontë are commemorated together on a tablet presented by the Brontë Society in 1947. Best known for their novels, they also jointly published a volume of verse in 1846, and Emily's poems continue to be read. The last poem she wrote begins:

No coward soul is mine,
No trembler in the world's storm-troubled sphere:
I see Heaven's glories shine,
And faith shines equal, arming me from fear.

Over the doorway leading into St Faith's Chapel there is a memorial by Nollekens to Oliver Goldsmith (*c*. 1730–74) carrying a Latin epitaph by Dr Johnson. On hearing of Goldsmith's death, Johnson wrote to Boswell:

> He died of fever, made, I am afraid, more violent by uneasiness of mind. His debts began to be heavy, and all his resources were exhausted. Sir Joshua Reynolds is of opinion that he owed no less than two thousand pounds. Was ever poet so trusted before?

He was buried in the Temple Churchyard. Walter Scott (1771–1832) and William Makepeace Thackeray (1811–63) are mainly known for their novels, but they both also wrote verse. Scott's bust is near Goldsmith's monument, and Thackeray's in the adjacent west wall by the big statue of Joseph Addison (1672–1719) made by Richard Westmacott in 1809. Addison was buried in the Chapel of Henry VII. The historian, Thomas Macaulay, commented that considering Addison's popularity it was strange that it took so long for a memorial to be erected, but he approved the statue which

> represents him, as we can conceive him, clad in his dressing-gown, and freed from his wig, stepping from his parlour at Chelsea into his trim little garden . . .

Primarily famous for his essays, Addison's poetry included a celebration in heroic couplets of the victory of the English over the French at the Battle of Blenheim.

Not far away on the floor, near a tablet to Charles Dickens, are memorials to Rudyard Kipling (1865–1936) and Thomas Hardy (1840–1928). Although both are probably best known for their prose, Kipling's ballads were particularly popular when poetry reading was a regular domestic entertainment (and several of them were set to music), and Hardy himself preferred his own poetry to his novels. The circumstances of Hardy's burial were bizarre. He had stated in his will that he wished to be buried in

Stinsford, Dorset, near his parents and first wife. But when the offer of burial in the Abbey was made, his second wife decided to have his heart removed and buried at Stinsford, while the rest of his body went to Westminster – being cremated at Woking on the way. Kipling was one of his pall-bearers. An elderly Dorset woman is reported to have remarked about the affair: 'And when day of Judgement be come, Almighty, 'e'll say: " 'Ere be 'eart, but where be rest of 'e?" '. On a more serious note, Hardy's poem *Afterwards* meditates on what might be said of him after his death – this is one verse:

> If, when hearing that I have been stilled at last, they stand at
>   the door,
>   Watching the full-starred heavens that winter sees,
> Will this thought rise on those who will meet my face no more,
>   'He was one who had an eye for such mysteries'?

In the next cluster of floor tablets, near the ornate memorials which include the actor David Garrick's, is one marking the grave of Sir William D'Avenant (1606–68), who succeeded Ben Jonson as poet laureate, and who was given an imitative accolade: 'O rare Sr William Davenant'. A Cavalier, he was buried in the grave from which his Roundhead rival for the laureateship had been cast out at the Restoration. Shakespeare used to lodge at D'Avenant's parents' inn in Oxford, and it is said that William may have been his son. On a column not far from the eastern entrance to Poets' Corner there is a bust of William Blake (1757–1827) by Jacob Epstein which was placed there in 1957 to commemorate Blake's bicentenary.

Leaving Poets' Corner and entering the east cloister, at the bottom of the wooden ramp there is a stone which marks the grave of Aphra Behn (1640–89), poet, playwright and novelist. Remarkable as one of the first women to earn a living as an author, she also contributed the first anti-slavery work to English literature in her novel *Oroonoko*. Her most considerable poem was a coronation ode to James II. Further along the east cloister is the entrance to the chapter house, on the right of which is a window, with a portrait head below, to the poet and editor James Russell Lowell (1819–91) who was Minister of the United States in London for five years. His poetry includes *A Fable for Critics* and he was the first editor of the *Atlantic Monthly*.

In St Margaret's Church, which lies on the north side of the

Abbey, there is a memorial window to Sir Walter Ralegh (*c*. 1552–1618) which was donated by Americans in 1882 and carries an inscription by Lowell. The window shows Ralegh leaving England and landing in America, and includes among other figures those of Edmund Spenser and Elizabeth I. Ralegh was executed in Old Palace Yard and spent his last night in the Gatehouse which used to stand in front of the entrance to the Abbey. Richard Lovelace (1618–58) was also confined there, and during his imprisonment wrote the poem containing the lines

Stone walls do not a prison make,
  Nor iron bars a cage.

Miniature painting of Sir Walter Ralegh by Nicholas Hilliard. 'He was a tall, handsome, and bold man: but . . . damnable proud' (John Aubrey). (*National Portrait Gallery*)

17

Ralegh's body was buried in St Margaret's, but according to one account

> his Head was long preserv'd in a case by his Widow, who surviv'd him twenty-nine years, and after her Death by his Son Carew, with whom it is said to have been buried at West Horsley in Surrey.

The memorial window to Milton was donated by G. W. Childs of Philadelphia and was unveiled by Matthew Arnold in 1888. The window shows incidents from Milton's life and scenes from *Paradise Lost* and *Paradise Regained*. It is also a memorial to Milton's second wife and their child: he married her in St Margaret's in 1656, and buried her and the baby there a year later. G. W. Childs is himself commemorated by a memorial window in the nave of the Abbey which includes the figures of William Cowper (1731–1800) and George Herbert (1593–1633). Herbert stands in clerical dress above lines taken from the last verse of his poem *The Church Porch*. Cowper is depicted in cap and dressing-gown with one of his pet hares; he is holding a picture of his mother, who died when he was six, and lines are quoted from his poem *On the Receipt of My Mother's Picture out of Norfolk*. It was written when he was fifty-nine and had been sent a picture of his mother by a cousin.

On the south side of the Abbey, and approached through Dean's Yard, are the buildings of Westminster School, an ancient monastic school which was refounded by Elizabeth I. It is still flourishing today, and its past pupils include Ben Jonson, George Herbert, John Dryden, Matthew Prior, William Cowper, Charles Churchill and Robert Southey. Poor Cowper, a shy and melancholy child, had a most miserable time at the boarding school to which he was sent immediately after his mother died, but is said to have been happier at Westminster. Nevertheless in later life he wrote a long poem *Tirocinium; or, a review of Schools* with the aim of 'recommending private tuition in preference to an education at school'. It contains these lines which still strike a relevant note:

> There shall he learn, ere sixteen winters old,
> That authors are most useful, pawn'd or sold;
> That pedantry is all that schools impart,
> But taverns teach the knowledge of the heart;

There waiter Dick, with bacchanalian lays,
Shall win his heart and have his drunken praise
His counsellor and bosom friend shall prove,
And some street-pacing harlot his first love.
Schools, unless discipline were doubly strong,
Detain their adolescent charge too long;
The management of tyros of eighteen
Is difficult, their punishment obscene.

It is reported that Charles Churchill (1731–64), at the age of fifteen, 'having by some misdemeanour displeased his masters, was compelled to compose and recite in the schoolroom a poetical declamation in Latin. . . . This he accomplished in a masterly manner.' Three years later he clandestinely married, and in 1758 succeeded his father as curate of St John's, Smith Square, near Westminster School. This is a very beautiful baroque church now used as a concert hall. He preached his father's old sermons, and while acting as tutor in a girls' seminary in Bloomsbury 'his habits were so irregular that he was compelled to resign both his church and his school'. He was a great theatre-goer and became well known through his satire on contemporary actors, *The Rosciad*. Robert Southey is said to have 'made little progress in school learning but nourished his mind with out-of-the-way reading'. When he was eighteen he was expelled because of an essay called 'The Flagellant' which he had written and published in the school magazine, and which argued against the excessive flogging prevalent at the time.

The Houses of Parliament are not immediately linked with poetry, though members of both houses have included poets and versifiers. In present times the Earl of Gowrie, a member of the House of Lords (and the 1979 Thatcher government), is a published poet; and Norman Buchan, MP, lightened the Scottish devolution debate by publishing his verse pamphlet *The MacDunciad* – with due acknowledgement to Pope (and Byron). Byron himself entered the political arena in 1812 when he gave his maiden speech in the House of Lords urging members to oppose a bill bringing in the death penalty for the Luddites – workers who broke the machines and burned the mills of employers who aggravated poverty and unemployment. He declared

I have been in some of the most oppressed provinces of

Turkey, but never under the most despotic of infidel
governments did I behold such squalid wretchedness as I
have seen since my return in the very heart of a Christian
country. How can you carry the Bill into effect? Can you
commit a whole country to their own prisons? Will you erect
a gibbet in every field, and hang up men like scarecrows?

As a result of his speech he was included on the committee which
recommended reducing the death penalty to a fine or
imprisonment, but when the bill went back to the House of
Commons the death penalty was restored.

Probably the only time that poetry has ever itself been the
subject of a parliamentary debate was on 22 November 1978 in the
House of Lords when Lord (Ted) Willis introduced as his subject
'The conditions of poets and poetry in Britain'. Himself a
dramatist and novelist, and then President of the Writers' Guild of
Great Britain, Willis wanted to air both the importance of poetry
to the imaginative life of the nation and the fact that he felt more
money should be spent on it. It was a good-natured debate,
lasting two and a half hours, and combining elements of
perspicacity, passion, common sense, eccentricity and sheer
muddle-headedness. Viscount Eccles summed up the problem
that taxes many people when discussing patronage of the arts:

I am sorry to say that it appears that some modern poets do
not want to earn a living other than by writing poetry. I have
often been astonished at the number of artists and writers
who appear to think that society owes them a living,
irrespective of the quality of their work.

It is a problem that brooks no real answer, and provides us with a
brief opportunity to see how the place of the poet in society has
changed.

In Chaucer's day the court provided him with both jobs and
patronage for his poetry. Not that either type of support was
remotely secure, being subject to political change and personal
whim. But on the whole, the fabric of his life seemed to be
integrated: administration, diplomacy, religion, law, philosophy, social behaviour – all were within his experience and
subjects for thought and expression. Yet his most famous work,
The Canterbury Tales, was started during a period when he was
deprived of office, proving perhaps that his various jobs sapped

Lord (Ted) Willis, novelist and dramatist, who in 1978 originated a debate in the House of Lords on the state of British poetry. (*BBC Pictorial Publicity Library*)

his creative energy. And his poem *The House of Fame* (a dream allegory in which a golden eagle carries Chaucer in his talons while lecturing him on diverse subjects) contains a passage in which the eagle disparagingly remarks that Chaucer only re-wrote the plots of old love stories, and did not even know the gossip about his neighbours because

> For when thy labour doon al ys,
> And hast mad allë thy rekenyngës,
> In stede of reste and newë thyngës,
> Thou goost hom to thy hous anoon,
> And, also domb as any stoon,
> Thou sittest at another book
> Tyl fully daswed ys thy look . . .

'Daswed' is dazed, and the 'rekenyngës' refer to the reckonings he had to make when he was Comptroller of Customs and

Subsidy of Wools, Skins and Tanned Hides in London. Besides at one time being Clerk of the King's Works, his other posts included Justice of the Peace, and Knight of the Shire for Kent. Today no artist could spread his net quite so wide. Contemporary poets such as Philip Larkin (b. 1922) and Roy Fuller (b. 1912) perform responsible jobs and develop their literary output, while others get brief respites with fellowships and grants and then hustle for journalistic commissions and teaching stints. But in both cases there is an element of fragmentation in the image of a poet's life because poetry itself has become a fringe activity. For hundreds of years after Chaucer, poets depended on being favourably received at court – occasionally switching allegiance from one ruler to another if political circumstances necessitated. Elizabeth II wields no such power of patronage, and the committees which dole out grants are by their nature faceless and tend to rouse criticism – albeit much of it ill-informed.

Lord Eccles may be right that society does not 'owe' poets a living, but Lord Willis spoke for many when he described their importance:

> There are times when the poet's vision is unique, when he sees farther and deeper than the politician and the businessman or the sociologist. At his best the poet is an engineer of the human soul, expressing . . . our fears and hopes, our pleasures and our tragedies in a way that sometimes makes the heart throb like a drum.

> Perhaps because it is so difficult to put into words what I am trying to say I may try to illustrate what I mean by example. Suppose I were to say to your Lordships something like this:

> > The aging process will not, of course, affect these men and women in the same way as it affects other men and women. But memory-wise they will remain in an on-going situation.

> If I said that to your Lordships you . . . would certainly not remember a single word of it. But put the same thought in the mind of the poet and you get something that millions of people will never forget:

> > They shall grow not old, as we that are left grow old:
> > Age shall not weary them, nor the years condemn.
> > At the going down of the sun and in the morning
> > We will remember them.

(from For the Fallen by Laurence Binyon)

. . . I should like to add one further point before coming to more practical thoughts. If you wish to know which way the wind is blowing in Britain, if you wish to know how our young people think and feel, then buy, read and listen to the work of our young modern poets. You may not like the style, you may think it awkward and exaggerated, not at all what you expect of poetry. Indeed, some of it is rubbish. But the best of the poets writing today have a true vision, and we should do well to listen to their voices.

There will, of course, always be those who do not agree with such sentiments, who will side with George II who said:

Who is this [Alexander] Pope that I hear so much about? I cannot discover what is his merit. Why will not my subjects write in prose? I hear a great deal, too, of Shakespeare, but I cannot read him, he is such a *bombast* fellow.

CHAPTER 2

Southwark

George II was not the only man to accuse Shakespeare of writing bombast – Dryden did too. But with Dryden we get the full picture, an intimation of what turns part of Southwark into hallowed ground. It is a ramshackle, neglected, ill-planned area, but the fact that Shakespeare's plays were first performed there makes it unique. As Dryden explained:

> He was the man who of all modern, and perhaps ancient poets, had the largest and most comprehensive soul. . . . He was naturally learn'd; he needed not the spectacles of books to read Nature; he looked inwards, and found her there. . . . He is many times flat, insipid; his comic wit degenerating into clenches, his serious swelling into bombast. But he is always great, when some occasion is presented to him.

The part of Southwark that concerns us lies near the river, around Bankside and Borough High Street. The gap between what once happened there and what may be seen today is enormous. But simply because it has not been totally transformed by modern developments (though these are continuously appearing), it is possible to reach quite far back into the past. The surroundings are not quaint or even attractive, but hints and memories emerge through the urban decay and muddle like dulled old coins in a ploughed field.

There are exceptions to the area's mixture of dilapidation and commercial brashness, of which Southwark Cathedral (or the Church of St Saviour and St Mary Overy) – just south of London Bridge – is the most outstanding. It is beautifully looked after, flourishes as a local centre for worship and music, and although much rebuilt has traces of its long history dating back to Norman times. And it has some interesting literary associations.

John Gower, Chaucer's contemporary, spent the last years of his life in the precincts of the cathedral (then known as the Church of St Mary Overy) and left it many gifts and bequests. He was married there in 1397, soon after going blind, and his tomb, which has been restored several times, is one of the finest monuments in the cathedral. Brightly painted in red, green, black and gold, it has an effigy of Gower wearing a long damask robe, and with his head resting upon his three main works: *Vox Clamantis*, *Speculum Meditantis*, and *Confessio Amantis* – which he wrote in Latin, French and English respectively.

It was from *Confessio Amantis* that Shakespeare (1564–1616) drew the plot of *Pericles, Prince of Tyre*, and the character who acts as Chorus in the play is actually called Gower and his speeches are written in the verse metre which Gower used. Although Shakespeare was living mainly in retirement in Stratford when he wrote the play, the effigy of Gower might have been particularly fresh in his mind since his youngest brother, Edmund, had very recently been buried in that church and he would presumably have attended the funeral. Edmund was an actor, and it is recorded that his burial was marked 'with a fore noone knell of the great bell'. The site of his grave is not known.

Shakespeare himself is commemorated in the cathedral by a full-length figure in alabaster (1911) reclining in front of a relief sculpture of Bankside as it was in his time. This includes the southern end of London Bridge where the heads of decapitated criminals were spiked over Bridge Gate. Not only was this then a familiar sight, but when Shakespeare was nineteen, one of his mother's relatives suffered such a fate after being involved in a Catholic conspiracy. There is also a stained-glass window (1954) showing characters from his plays. It was during Shakespeare's time that James I organized a new translation of the Bible, known as the Authorized Version. Fifty-four translators undertook the work, one of whom, Lancelot Andrewes (Bishop of Winchester), is buried in the cathedral. The translators consulted other experts, and the poetical sections – such as the Psalms and the Song of Solomon – were shown to literary men. Rudyard Kipling wrote a short story in which Shakespeare and Ben Jonson (1572–1637) discuss a problem presented to them by one of the translators; although there is no proof that such an incident took place, it is not totally unlikely.

Southwark Cathedral has a strong American connection in its Harvard Chapel, restored in 1907 in memory of John Harvard,

Mr. WILLIAM
SHAKESPEARES

COMEDIES,
HISTORIES, &
TRAGEDIES.

Published according to the True Originall Copies.

Martin Droeshout sculpsit London.

LONDON
Printed by Isaac Iaggard, and Ed. Blount. 1623.

Title page of the First Folio (1623) of Shakespeare's plays, with a portrait engraving by Martin Droeshout. Droeshout made the engraving five years after Shakespeare's death, and it is not known upon what original it was based. 'He was a handsome, well-shap't man; very good company, and of very readie and pleasant smooth witt' (John Aubrey). (*British Museum*)

founder of Harvard University, who was born in Southwark in 1607. The chapel contains a memorial tablet to Oscar Hammerstein II (1895–1960), and if this seems a massive jump from Shakespeare, perhaps one should remember that the ability to write words for musical settings was as popular in Elizabethan times as it is in ours. Members of an audience might come away singing

Under the greenwood tree
Who loves to lie with me

from *As You Like It*, as audiences of this century have recalled

Fish gotta swim, birds gotta fly,
I'm goin' to love one man till I die

from *Show Boat*. (And both lyricists have been included in the same programme when the incomparable Cleo Laine is in concert.) There is an unusual monument in the south transept of the cathedral which has a miniature effigy of William Emerson (d. 1575), a supposed ancestor of Ralph Waldo Emerson (1803–82).

Once outside the cathedral, order and cleanliness recede. Nineteenth-century warehouses, many now disused, dominate the area. In Clink Street the remains of a fourteenth-century great hall is embalmed in the side of a warehouse, and the name of the street reminds us that it once housed a prison for heretics as 'in the clink' survives as a slang expression for imprisonment. On Bankside, the splendid 'Anchor Inn', built in 1775, was a regular haunt of Dr Johnson. On the wall of a brewery in Park Street a plaque records that the Globe Theatre once stood nearby. This is where many of Shakespeare's plays were performed, and he was both a shareholder and a member of the group who acted there. Known as the wooden 'O' because of its shape, the Globe was burned down in 1613 when a stage-effect canon, used at the first performance of *Henry VIII*, caused its thatch roof to catch fire. Luckily no one was hurt (though one man's breeches had to be

A Looking-glaſſe

VVherein is to be ſeene many fearfull examples in the time of this grieuous Vi...
Country to be more pitifull

City and Countrey :

with an admonition to our Londoners flying from the City; and a perfwafion come for fuccor amongſt them.

Londoners flee from the plague; an illustration from a seventeenth-century broadsheet. Shakespeare was alive during the 1603 plague when theatres were closed and citizens moved to the country. In the Great Plague of 1665, the year before the Great Fire, a contemporary recorded: 'Now shops are shut in, people rare, and very few walk about . . . the long summer days are spent from morning until twilight in conveying the vast number of dead bodies . . . ' (*Society of Antiquaries*)

doused with 'pottle ale') and the theatre was rebuilt the following year. Rose Alley nearby marks the site of the Rose Theatre, where Shakespeare acted when he first came to London, and where his earliest plays were performed. Bear Gardens was originally the site of a bear garden combined with the Hope Theatre; bear-baiting was a popular sport, rightly criticized by Pepys as 'a rude and nasty pleasure'. Ben Jonson's *Bartholomew Fair* was first acted at the Hope, a farcical play presenting scenes from the holiday fair which used to be held in the churchyard of St Bartholomew's Priory, Smithfield. In 1972 the Bear Gardens

An engraving (*c.* 1612) of the Globe Theatre, Southwark, where many of Shakespeare's plays were performed. (*Longman Picture Library*)

Museum was opened in an old warehouse, and it contains an interesting permanent exhibition relating to the Elizabethan theatre. Although run on a shoe-string, it is well worth visiting for an impression of the buildings and activities of Shakespeare's time, and it has an excellent model of one of the frost fairs that used to be held on the Thames when it froze right across.

The 'Falcon Inn' at the east end of Bankside occupies the site of the Swan Theatre, the third of the trio of famous Elizabethan theatres in the area. In the summer of 1596 its owner, Francis Langley, was accused with Shakespeare of threatening the life of William Gardner, a justice of the peace in Southwark of bad reputation. The charge was probably unjustified, and it meant the burden of a lawsuit in a summer darkened by the death of Shakespeare's son, Hamnet. He was trying to write *King John*, and the words of Constance, mother of the doomed Arthur, carry special meaning:

> Grief fills the room up of my absent child,
> Lies in his bed, walks up and down with me,
> Puts on his pretty looks, repeats his words,
> Remembers me of all his gracious parts,
> Stuffs out his vacant garments with his form.

Returning westwards to Borough High Street, it is hard to imagine that the latter was once the main medieval route to Canterbury. A plaque on the wall of Talbot Court (now a service entrance for Guy's Hospital) is all that remains to record the site of the 'Tabard Inn', the place where Chaucer's pilgrims in *The Canterbury Tales* met at the start of their journey. It was, Chaucer recorded in the *Prologue*, a 'gentil hostelrye', with generous-sized rooms and stables. Present-day visitors need not, however, despair of finding a decent hostelry for themselves in the High Street, since in the courtyard just north of Talbot Court lies the 'George Inn', a National Trust property dating from 1676. It is the only galleried inn left in London, and has miraculously escaped modernization. The benches, tables, beams and fireplaces are all genuinely old, and there is a 1797 Act of Parliament clock: one of the communal clocks built to avoid individual tax on watches. In summer, Shakespeare plays are sometimes performed in the courtyard. Nearby, White Hart Yard marks the site of the 'White Hart Inn' mentioned by the rebel Jack Cade in Shakespeare's *Henry VI*, Part 2.

Shakespeare players in the courtyard of the 'George Inn', Borough High Street, Southwark, 1947. This seventeenth-century pub (on the left) is the last surviving galleried inn in London. (*Press Association Ltd*)

Further south along Borough High Street, on the same side as the 'George Inn', are the sites of two prisons with literary associations. The Old Marshalsea prison was situated near the entrance to Mermaid Court, and in 1605 Ben Jonson, George Chapman (*c*. 1559–1634) the poet, translator and dramatist, and John Marston (*c*. 1575–1634) dramatist, were briefly imprisoned together for their collaboration on the play *Eastward hoe* which slighted the Scots, thereby upsetting James I. The story goes that Jonson imprisoned himself voluntarily, and after his release gave a banquet to his friends in the middle of which

> his old mother drank to him, and shewed him a paper which she had (if the sentence had taken execution) to have mixed in the prison among his drink, which was full of lusty strong poison; and that she was no churl, she told him she minded first to have drunk of it herself.

31

King's Bench Prison used to stand near the entrance to Angel Place, and Thomas Dekker (*c.* 1570–1632) was confined there for five years for debt. He wrote plays for the Rose Theatre in collaboration with Jonson and others, and one of his lyrics has remained a popular lullaby:

> Golden slumbers kiss your eyes,
> Smiles awake you when you rise . . .

It received its widest audience when sung by Paul McCartney in the Beatles' album *Abbey Road*.

The Church of St George the Martyr (which is not always open), on the junction of Borough High Street and Long Lane, has strong connections with Charles Dickens, and its one poetic connection is with the now somewhat obscure Nahum Tate (1652–1715) who is buried there. He was poet laureate, and was pilloried in Pope's satire *The Dunciad*. He wrote a watered-down adaptation of *King Lear* (in which Cordelia survives and marries Edgar) which was performed for many years. His words are still heard today in the libretto to Purcell's *Dido and Aeneas* and the carol 'While shepherds watch'd their flocks by night' (written in collaboration with Nicholas Brady, and readily parodied by generations of schoolchildren). The Church of St George represents the point of penetration into Southwark where all but the most zealous might begin to retrace their steps, though a few more sites should be mentioned.

Opposite the church Marshalsea Road leads into Mint Street where W. H. Davies (1871–1940) stayed in a lodging house called the Farm House (now demolished), recalled in his poem *An Old House in London*:

> In fancy I can see thee stand
> Again in the green meadow-land;
> As in thine infancy, long past,
> When Southwark was a lovely waste;
> And larks and blackbirds sang around . . .
> . . . Instead of those green meadows, now
> Three hundred hungry children show
> Rags and white faces at thy door
> For charity. We see no more
> Green lanes, but alleys dark instead . . .

At the bottom of Mint Street is Leigh Hunt Street, commemorating the nearby site of yet another prison, Horsemonger Lane Gaol where Leigh Hunt (1784–1859) was held for two years for calling the Prince Regent 'a fat Adonis of 50'. However he received frequent visits from his friends, who included Byron and Charles Lamb, and continued to edit the paper in which the libel had appeared. He wrote this enchanting description of his cell:

I papered the walls with a trellis of roses; I had the ceiling coloured with clouds and sky; the barred windows were

Leigh Hunt's cell in Horsemonger Lane Gaol, Southwark, as imagined by Wendy Dowson from Hunt's written description.

screened with Venetian blinds; and when my bookcases were
set up, with their busts and flowers, and a pianoforte made
its appearance, perhaps there was not a handsomer room on
that side of the water. I took a pleasure, when a stranger
knocked at the door, to see him come in and stare about him.
The surprise on issuing from the borough and passing
through the avenue of a jail was dramatic. Charles Lamb
declared there was no other such room except in a fairy tale.

Scovell Road (a short walk south from Leigh Hunt Street) is
near the site of the final (demolished) prison in the area to have
housed a poet. The King's Bench Prison moved there in 1758, and
Christopher Smart (1722–71) was imprisoned for debt and died
there. He had previously been confined in an asylum – a
punishment Dr Johnson thought excessive:

My poor friend Smart showed the disturbance of his mind by
falling upon his knees and saying his prayers in the street, or
in any other unusual place. Now although, rationally
speaking, it is greater madness not to pray at all than to pray
as Smart did, I am afraid there are so many who do not pray,
that their understanding is not called in question. . . . His
infirmities were not noxious to society. He insisted on people
praying with him; and I'd as lief pray with Kit Smart as
anyone else . . .

These are lines from Smart's must for all cat lovers,

For I Will Consider My Cat Jeoffrey:

For first he looks upon his fore-paws to see if they are clean.

For secondly he kicks up behind to clear away there.
For thirdly he works it upon stretch with the fore-paws
    extended.

For fourthly he sharpens his paws by wood.
For fifthly he washes himself.
For sixthly he rolls upon wash.
For seventhly he fleas himself, that he may not be interrupted
    upon the beat.

For eighthly he rubs himself against a post.
For ninthly he looks up for his instructions.
For tenthly he goes in quest of food.

Returning back towards London Bridge station, Guy's Hospital (in Thomas Street) reminds us that John Keats (1795–1821) used to lodge in Dean Street (now demolished under a railway arch) when he was working as a dresser at the hospital. In October 1816 he went to visit a friend in Clerkenwell and they sat up all night reading and discussing Chapman's translation of Homer (the same Chapman who had been imprisoned with Ben Jonson). Keats walked back to his lodgings at dawn, and immediately wrote the sonnet *On First Looking into Chapman's Homer*, beginning 'Much have I travell'd in the realms of gold'.

A twentieth-century poet, Richard Church (1893–1972), who often used to cross London Bridge

> Among commuters by the million;
> Part of that long, black caterpillar
> Nosing northward every morning,
> Slipping southward every night . . .

was always intrigued by Hay's Wharf, the large warehouse on the south-east side of the bridge. He remembered how as a boy the scents emanating from it

> . . . coffee berries, orris-root,
> Nine-and-twenty kinds of tea,
> Geranium oil, and oil of pine . . .

would make him imagine coming

> To land beyond the coral reefs
> Where all adventurers have longed
> To voyage through the innocent years . . .

The present London Bridge was rebuilt between 1967 and 1973, the 1825–31 version (used by Richard Church) having been carefully dismantled and shipped to Arizona. Before that, 100 feet down stream, there was a wooden bridge, which until 1729 was the only bridge across the Thames in London. During Shakespeare's time it was not only a display site for criminals' severed heads, but also a street with wooden houses on either side and a chapel. He would have walked over it leaving the Globe on his way to meet friends in the 'Mermaid Tavern', and in its different way it would have been as busy as the London Bridge

described by Richard Church. Later, when Shakespeare left his
friends and went to his house in Silver Street, perhaps he had an
hour of solitude before sleep during which he forgot the triumphs
and tribulations of the theatre and turned his mind to the
expression of his most private feelings. It was Wordsworth who
described the sonnet form as the 'key' with which 'Shakespeare
unlocked his heart', and it was lines like these that moved him to
do so:

> Shall I compare thee to a summer's day?
> Thou art more lovely and more temperate.
> Rough winds do shake the darling buds of May,
> And summer's lease hath all too short a date:
> Sometime too hot the eye of heaven shines,
> And often is his gold complexion dimm'd;
> And every fair from fair sometime declines,
> By chance, or nature's changing course, untrimm'd;
> But thy eternal summer shall not fade
> Nor lose possession of that fair thou ow'st;
> Nor shall Death brag thou wand'rest in his shade,
> When in eternal lines to time thou grow'st.
>> So long as men can breathe or eyes can see,
>> So long lives this, and this gives life to thee.

CHAPTER 3

The City

'The stones of St Paul's flew like grenades, and the lead melted down the streets in a stream. The very pavements glowed with fiery redness, and neither horse nor man was able to tread on them.' This is the diarist, John Evelyn, describing the destruction of St Paul's Cathedral in the Great Fire of London which raged for three days in September 1666. John Dryden (1631–1700) recalled how Charles II came to help his citizens:

> Now day appears and with the day the king
> Whose early care had robbed him of his rest.
> Far off the cracks of falling houses ring
> And shrieks of subjects pierce his tender breast.

Two and a half centuries later the Blitz wreaked the second major catastrophe on the City. Again the king, this time George VI, stayed to support his people. Edith Sitwell (1887–1964) described the 1940 bombing in images of the crufixion:

> Still falls the Rain –
> Dark as the world of man, black as our loss –
> Blind as the nineteen hundred and forty nails
> Upon the Cross.

These two holocausts divide the architectural history of the City into three very distinct main phases: medieval, Wren, and modern. Very little of the first remains; Wren's restored churches – and of course, St Paul's – provide the visitor's mainstay and miracle; and about the modern phase it is difficult not to have very mixed feelings indeed. It is also difficult to glimpse the City poets through the concrete, since the chief ones – Donne and Milton – belong to a much earlier time.

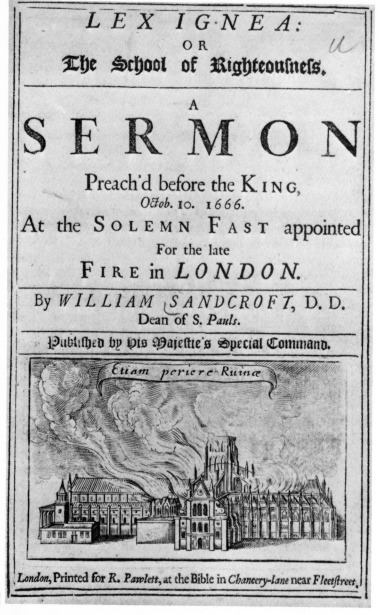

LEX IGNEA:
OR
𝕿𝔥𝔢 𝔖𝔠𝔥𝔬𝔬𝔩 𝔬𝔣 𝔕𝔦𝔤𝔥𝔱𝔢𝔬𝔲𝔰𝔫𝔢𝔰𝔰.

A
SERMON

Preach'd before the KING,
Octob. 10. 1666.
At the SOLEMN FAST appointed
For the late
FIRE in *LONDON*.

By *WILLIAM SANDCROFT*, D.D.
Dean of S. *Pauls.*

𝔓𝔲𝔟𝔩𝔦𝔰𝔥𝔢𝔡 𝔟𝔶 𝔥𝔦𝔰 𝔐𝔞𝔧𝔢𝔰𝔱𝔦𝔢'𝔰 𝔖𝔭𝔢𝔠𝔦𝔞𝔩 𝔠𝔬𝔪𝔪𝔞𝔫𝔡.

Etiam periere Ruinæ

London, Printed for *R. Pawlett,* at the Bible in *Chancery-lane* near *Fleetstreet.*

Title page of the sermon preached before Charles II after the Great Fire, showing the old St Paul's Cathedral in full blaze. 'It made me weep to see it. The churches, houses, and all on fire and flaming at once, and a horrid noise the flames made, and the cracking of houses at their ruin' (Samuel Pepys). (*London Library*)

38

St Paul's Cathedral in the Blitz, 1940. (*Popperfoto*)

For the last ten years of his life, John Donne (*c.* 1572–1631) was Dean of St Paul's – the old St Paul's that is, a great gothic cathedral which by then lacked its soaring lead and timber spire, struck by lightning several years before he was born. Donne has become one of the favourite poets of our century, for he understood well the contradictions of lust and love, and the conflict between worldly ambition and spiritual need. Perhaps the most powerful image of Donne's London, which may still be seen, is his own memorial in St Paul's – the only one to survive the Great Fire intact, and now placed in the south choir aisle. Carved in stone, it shows Donne, wrapped in a shroud, standing on an urn awaiting the resurrection of the body. According to Izaak Walton this was entirely Donne's own idea. Knowing he was near to death, he asked for a large wooden urn to be carved, a shroud to be brought, and an artist to attend. After being wrapped in the shroud so only his face showed, he stood on the urn with his eyes closed and bade the artist make a life-size sketch. From this Nicholas Stone later made the memorial carving. It was Donne who wrote:

No man is an island, entire of itself; every man is a piece of the continent, a part of the main. If a clod be washed away by the sea, Europe is the less, as well as if a promontory were, as well as if a manor of thy friend's or of thine own were. Any man's death diminishes me, because I am involved in mankind. And therefore never send to know for whom the bell tolls. It tolls for thee.

John Donne, by an unknown artist after a miniature by Isaac Oliver. 'He was of stature moderately tall, of a strait and equally-proportioned body, to which all his words and actions gave an unexpressible addition of Comeliness' (Izaak Walton). (*National Portrait Gallery*)

The subject of death leads us fairly logically to the Tower of London, which is the starting place for the route around the City taken in this chapter. It is not suggested that it should be slavishly followed, but it may be picked out on a map and those parts visited that are of special interest to the reader. The Tower itself is, of course, a major tourist attraction (i.e. crowds!), and might well take up a fair amount of time. Sir Thomas Wyatt (c. 1503–42), who introduced the sonnet form into England, was imprisoned in 1536, allegedly for having been Ann Boleyn's lover. After his release he was allowed to continue his former work as a diplomat for Henry VIII, but fell into disfavour again in 1540 and was sent to the Tower for three months 'for papist tendencies'. One of his poems, *The Lover sheweth how he is forsaken of such as he sometime enjoyed*, illustrates the passions and fickleness a courtier might encounter. It begins:

They flee from me, that sometime did me seke,
With naked fote stalkyng within my chamber.
Once have I seen them gentle, tame, and meke,
That now are wild, and do not once remember
That sometyme they have put them selves in danger,
To take bread at my hand, and now they range,
Busily sekyng in continuall change.

Sir Walter Ralegh (c. 1552–1618) was one of the Tower's most famous prisoners, and much of his poetry was written while he was imprisoned there. His first spell was in 1592, a punishment for having seduced one of Queen Elizabeth's maids of honour – whom he later married. It was then that he wrote the long elegy *Cynthia, the Lady of the Sea* expressing devotion to his queen. His second imprisonment, in the Bloody Tower, was for thirteen years when James I gaoled him on a confused charge of treason in order to appease Spain. During this time he was visited by 'the wits and poets, the scholars and inventors of his time' and in the Garden House adjoining the Bloody Tower 'he distilled essences and spirits, compounded his great cordial, discovered a method (afterwards lost) of turning salt water into sweet . . . invented the modern warship, and wrote his *History of the World*'. He was released in order to undertake an expedition to South America, and when that failed he was re-arrested and imprisoned again in the Tower before his execution at Westminster.

Sir William D'Avenant (1606–68), poet laureate under

Charles I, was imprisoned for two years under Cromwell and is said to have been saved by the intervention of Milton. When Milton himself, who had been Secretary for Foreign Tongues to Cromwell's Council of State, was endangered at the restoration of Charles II, D'Avenant is reported to have returned the favour. D'Avenant had the misfortune to lose his nose as the result of illness, and was the butt of many jokes from fellow writers.

John Wilmot, Earl of Rochester (1647–80), tends to be remembered as a libertine first and a poet second, his considerable gifts being overshadowed by his rakish behaviour. When he was eighteen he abducted an heiress and was imprisoned briefly in the Tower by Charles II. However he was soon released – his position at court swung violently between that of favourite and of miscreant – and later married the heiress. Once, when out of favour, he went to live anonymously in the City and disclosed and denounced the debaucheries of the king to the civic dignitaries. Later he set up as a quack doctor, with lodgings in Tower Street and a stall on Tower Hill from which he dispensed cosmetics and advice to gullible ladies. He died when he was thirty-three, and confessed that at one period he had been under the influence of drink for five consecutive years; however this did not impair his faculty for lyrical and satirical poetry. In *A Satyr Against Mankind* he wrote:

> Were I, who to my Cost already am
> One of those strange, prodigious Creatures *Man*,
> A Spirit free, to choose for my own Share,
> What sort of Flesh and Blood I pleas'd to wear,
> I'd be a Dog, a Monkey, or a Bear,
> Or any thing, but that vain Animal,
> Who is so proud of being Rational.

Rochester took a great interest in the theatre, and the playwright Samuel Pordage (of whom it is said he had 'at least rendered himself famous for following the Muses, though he could never overtake them') decided to send his rhymed heroic tragedy *Herod and Mariamne* to him in the hope of eliciting patronage. When Pordage finally recovered the manuscript it had written on its cover:

> Poet, who'er thou art, God damn thee,
> Go hang thyself, and burn thy Mariamne.

Rochester was responsible for training the great tragic actress Elizabeth Barry, who was his mistress, and who by coincidence was loved, unrequitedly, by the verse playwright Thomas Otway (1652–85) who is reported to have died tragically on Tower Hill. The story goes that he was destitute and starving in a public house, 'and being naked and in a rage of hunger, he went to a neighbouring coffee-house, and asked a gentleman for a shilling. The gentleman generously gave the starving poet a guinea, on which Otway rushed into the nearest baker's, bought a roll, and, eating with ravenous haste, was choked with the first mouthful'.

Custom House quay, down by the river off Lower Thames Street (where Chaucer probably lived while Comptroller of Customs), was where William Cowper came in deep depression with the intention of killing himself:

William Cowper by George Romney. Cowper, who suffered from mental depression, liked this drawing, noting in a sonnet addressed to Romney that 'symptoms none of woe / In thy incomparable work appear. / Well – I am satisfied it should be so'. (*National Portrait Gallery*)

Not knowing where to poison myself, for I was liable to continual interruption in my chambers, from my laundress and her husband, I laid aside that intention, and resolved upon drowning. For that purpose, I immediately took a coach, and ordered the man to drive to Tower Wharf; intending to throw myself into the river from the Custom House quay. . . . But upon coming to the quay, I found the water low, and a porter seated upon some goods there, as if on purpose to prevent me. This passage to the bottomless pit being mercifully shut against me, I returned back to the coach and ordered it to return to the Temple.

Turning west into Lower Thames Street, towards London Bridge, one comes to St Magnus Martyr, considered by T. S. Eliot to have 'one of the finest among Wren's interiors'; he encapsulated the area, which includes the former Billingsgate fish market, in *The Waste Land*:

O City city, I can sometimes hear
Beside a public bar in Lower Thames Street
The pleasant whining of a mandoline
And a clatter and a chatter from within
Where fishmen lounge at noon: where the walls
Of Magnus Martyr hold
Inexplicable splendour of Ionian white and gold.

At the top of Fish Street Hill the huge Monument commemorates the Great Fire which broke out in adjacent Pudding Lane. Dryden described the misery of people whose homes were burned down:

Those who have none sit round where once it was,
    And with full eyes each wonted room require;
Haunting the yet warm ashes of the place,
    As murder'd men walk where they did expire.

Up Gracechurch Street one reaches Lombard Street, in which Plough Court, on the left, has a plaque marking the site where Alexander Pope was born (1688) in a dwelling over his father's linen warehouse. At the point where Lombard Street meets King William Street is the church of St Mary Woolnoth, whose hexagonal clock is remembered by Eliot, again in *The Waste Land*:

Sighs, short and infrequent, were exhaled,
And each man fixed his eyes before his feet.
Flowed up the hill and down King William Street,
To where Saint Mary Woolnoth kept the hours
With a dead sound on the final stroke of nine.

On the opposite side of Lombard Street is Lloyds Bank (erected 1931) in whose predecessor Eliot worked from 1919 to 1922. I. A. Richards, the critic, recalls visiting Eliot in his office and seeing

> a figure stooping, very like a dark bird in a feeder, over a big table covered with all sorts and sizes of foreign correspondence. The big table almost entirely filled a little room under the street. Within a foot of our heads when we stood were the thick, green glass squares of the pavement on which hammered all but incessantly the heels of the passers-by . . .

St Mary Woolnoth, built by Nicholas Hawksmoor, is well worth a visit and is now established as a centre to combat the pressures of stress and anxiety. One of its most famous rectors, John Newton, a reformed slave trader, started to write a hymn book with Cowper, but the latter had to retire to a mental hospital when only forty of the 400 hymns were completed. In a comic verse-letter to Newton, Cowper dramatized a conversation between a pipe and a snuff-box. The pipe is speaking here:

> My breath is as sweet as the breath of blown roses,
>   While you are a nuisance where'er you appear;
> There is nothing but snivelling and blowing of noses,
>   Such a noise as turns any man's stomach to hear.

Past the Bank of England, Princes Street leads into Moorgate and there is a small turning on the right called Telegraph Street. This was once the site of Bell Alley and Great Bell Yard where Robert Bloomfield (1766–1823) worked as a ladies' shoemaker and wrote *The Farmer's Boy* – which sold 26,000 copies. Born in Suffolk, he was too small to be an effective farm worker, and was sent to London to learn a trade. The degradations of urban poverty made him look back nostalgically to rural poverty. There is a plaque commemorating him on Kent House. Continuing north up Moorgate, and just past the crossing with London Wall, there is a pub called the 'Moorgate' (No. 85) with a plaque high on the wall marking the site of Keats's birthplace. In those days (1795) it was occupied by livery stables called the Swan and Hoop, run by Keats's father.

Leaving Finsbury Square on the right, and going into City Road, one comes to Bunhill Fields, which was used as a burial ground from 1623 to 1852. John Bunyan (author of *The Pilgrim's Progress*) is buried here, and the poet Robert Southey remarked: 'People like to be buried in company, and in good company. The Dissenters regarded Bunhill Fields' Burial ground as their *campo santo* [cemetary]. . . . ' William Blake (1757–1827), dissenter in the widest sense, was buried here; the site of the grave is unknown, but in 1927 a stone (which stands near Daniel Defoe's monument) was erected to both him and his wife. A modern poet, Julian Ennis, describes his pilgrimage to Bunyan's grave:

> Pelted by pigeons, the end of his nose
> Still chipped off by a splinter from the war,
> All boxed in by high glass and concrete,
> John Bunyan lies, a mouldering stone,
> Not much to come for all this wintry way . . .

Adrian Mitchell, who performs his own poems of social protest with great power. This drawing shows him standing by William Blake's memorial stone in Bunhill Fields, EC1. Mitchell has written a play about Blake called *Tyger, Tyger*.

NEAR BY LIE THE REMAINS OF
THE POET-PAINTER
WILLIAM BLAKE
1757 — 1827
AND OF HIS WIFE
CATHERINE SOPHIA
1762 — 1831

Bunhill Fields is not exactly a visitors' mecca, but despite Ennis's reservations it is a pleasant breathing space away from traffic. The path through leads to Bunhill Row, formerly Artillery Walk, where John Milton lived from 1662 until his death in 1674. (The house, which was No. 125, is demolished.) It was here he finished *Paradise Lost* and wrote *Paradise Regained* while totally blind, 'read to and written for by friends, daughters, hired men or other assistants of varying degrees of usefulness'. An early biographer (1734) describes the setting:

> I have heard . . . he Us'd to Sit in a grey Coarse Cloth Coat at the Door of his House near Bun-hill Fields. . . . In Warm Sunny Weather received the Visits of People of Distinguish'd Parts, as well as Quality. Lately I had . . . Another Picture of him from an Ancient Clergy-man. . . . He found him in a Small House, he thinks but One Room on a Floor; . . . he found John Milton sitting in an Elbow Chair, Black Cloaths, and Neat enough, Pale, but not Cadaverous, his Hands and Fingers Gouty . . .

The proximity of Blake's grave and Milton's last home makes the retelling of a delightful, but probably apocryphal, anecdote linking the two poets irresistible. At one point in their lives, William and Catherine Blake lived in a pretty house (now demolished) in Lambeth, complete with a garden. A friend is said to have called on them one day and found them in the summer-house, naked, reciting lines from *Paradise Lost*. 'Come in!' Blake cried; 'it's only Adam and Eve, you know!' Milton's Adam and Eve were described as inhabiting the Garden of Eden in 'Simplicity and spotless innocence!' – a not unapt phrase to apply to the Blakes. Milton continued:

> So pass'd they naked on, nor shunn'd the sight
> Of God or angel; for they thought no ill:
> So hand in hand they pass'd, the loveliest pair
> That ever since in love's embraces met.

Milton is buried in St Giles' Cripplegate Church, which may be reached by walking south down Bunhill Row into Moor Lane, and turning right into Fore Street. The church is marooned (or sensitively preserved, according to one's viewpoint) in the modern development of the Barbican. Still unfinished (1979), it is easy to lose one's way in this concrete environment where ramps and walkways seem to converge and end at random, and the high dwelling blocks present their already darkly-stained façades. In a poem called *A View of the Barbican*, David Wright (b. 1920) describes them as 'The angular fungi of our time.' It may be that when the area is finished, with the ambitious arts centre which will include the Royal Shakespeare Company's new theatre, it will seem more hospitable. The modern and unsightly Fore Street marks the position of one end of the now demolished Milton Street, which was once the original Grub Street, home of penniless hack authors. Walter Thornbury, in his Victorian narrative of London, deplored the change of name:

> The old Grub Street, the haunt of poor authors . . . has now changed its name to Milton Street. This absurd transition from Lazarus to Dives, from the dunghill to the palace, originated in the illogical remembrance of some dull-headed Government official that Milton died at his house in Artillery Walk. . . . The direct association of Pope's Grub Street poets [satirized in *The Dunciad*] was surely better . . . but officials are always the same. Here poor hacks of weak will and mistaken ambition sat up in bed, with blankets skewered about them, and, encouraged by gin, scribbled epics and lampoons, and fulsome dedications to purse-proud patrons.

According to a disputed account made by one P. Neve in his 'Narrative of the Disinterment of Milton's coffin', the poet's coffin was found and opened during church repairs in 1790. Neve gives this graphic and ghoulish description:

> Holmes, the journeyman, having fetched a mallet and a chisel, and cut open the top of the coffin, slantwise from the head, as low as the breast, so that, the top being doubled backward, they could see the corpse, he cut it open also at the foot. Upon first view of the body, it appeared perfect, and completely enveloped in the shroud, which was of many folds, the ribs standing up regularly. When they disturbed the shroud the ribs fell. Mr Fountain confessed that he pulled hard at the teeth, which resisted, until some one hit them a knock with a stone, when they easily came out. There were but five in the upper jaw, which were all perfectly sound and white, and all taken by Mr Fountain. He gave one of them to

Mr Laming. Mr Laming also took one from the lower jaw; and Mr Taylor took two from it. Mr Laming said that he had at one time a mind to bring away the whole under-jaw with the teeth in it; he had it in his hand, but tossed it back again. Also, that he lifted up the head, and saw a great quantity of hair, which lay strait and even, behind the head, and in the state of hair which had been combed and tied together before interment; but it was wet, the coffin having considerable corroded holes, both at the head and foot, and a great part of the water with which it had been washed on the Tuesday afternoon having run into it.

Cowper was horrified by this story, and wrote *Stanzas on the Late Indecent Liberties Taken with the Remains of Milton*, from which this is taken:

Ill fare the hands that heaved the stones
   Where Milton's ashes lay,
That trembled not to grasp his bones
   And steal his dust away!

The Museum of London, at the south-west corner of the Barbican, rightly attracts large crowds, and will supply rich visual information to flesh out in a visitor's mind images of historical poets' London. At the corner of Aldermanbury and Love Lane a small garden marks the site of the bombed church of St Mary Aldermanbury, which was removed in 1966 to Fulton, Missouri, as a memorial to Winston Churchill. Perhaps he may be allowed a corner in poets' London since his most famous speeches, like this one delivered to the House of Commons on 4 June 1940, were learned by heart and recited many times, in the manner of a poem – or a prayer.

We shall not flag or fail. We shall fight in France, we shall fight on the seas and oceans, we shall fight with growing confidence and growing strength in the air, we shall defend our island, whatever the cost may be, we shall fight on the beaches, we shall fight on the landing grounds, we shall fight in the fields and in the streets, we shall fight in the hills; we shall never surrender.

St Giles without Cripplegate, Barbican, where John Milton is buried.

Churchill once wrote that one of the advantages of being kept for so long in the lowest form at his school, where he was not a distinguished pupil, was that 'I got into my bones the essential structure of the normal British sentence – which is a noble thing.' Shakespeare probably once lived near Aldermanbury in Silver Street (demolished) and there is a memorial bust to him in the garden which also commemorates the editors of the first folio of his plays. Aldermanbury leads past the new Guildhall Library to Guildhall, whose remaining medieval origins are carefully

Ben Jonson, after a painting by A. Van Blijenberch. 'Jonson is described as wearing a loose coachman's coat, frequenting the Mermaid Tavern, where he drank seas of Canary, then reeling home to bed, and after a profuse perspiration, arising to his dramatic studies' (Walter Scott). (*National Portrait Gallery*)

preserved amid the restorations needed after the Great Fire and
the Blitz. The library has a vast collection of works on London,
and contains the deed signed by Shakespeare in 1613 for the
purchase of a house in Blackfriars. Milton is depicted in a
stained-glass window, and there are busts of Chaucer and
Tennyson on the stairs.

King Street leads down to Cheapside, where Keats lodged
during 1817, the year his first collection of poems was published.
(The building, No. 76, is now demolished.) He had stopped
working at Guy's Hospital, announcing to a friend: 'I find I
cannot exist without poetry – without eternal Poetry – half the
day will not do. . . . ' His lodgings were barely more than a
stone's throw from Bread Street, which has some of the richest
poetical associations of all London streets – a fact of which Keats
was well aware. Not only were Donne and Milton both born
there, but the famous 'Mermaid Tavern', frequented by Ralegh,
Jonson, Marlowe, Shakespeare, Donne, and many others, stood
near the junction of Bread Street and Cheapside. Unfortunately
no visual echoes of these associations have survived, and we
must make do with the playwright Francis Beaumont's evocative
lines taken from a letter he wrote to Ben Jonson:

> What things have we seen,
> Done at the Mermaid! heard words that have been
> So nimble, and so full of subtle flame,
> As if every one from whence they came,
> Had meant to put his whole wit in a jest,
> And had resolv'd to live a fool, the rest
> Of his dull life.

Two hundred years later, Keats nostalgically addressed the
departed company of poets that used to meet there:

> Souls of Poets dead and gone,
> What Elysium have ye known,
> Happy field or mossy cavern,
> Choicer than the Mermaid Tavern?
> Have ye tippled drink more fine
> Than mine host's Canary wine?
> Or are fruits of Paradise
> Sweeter than those dainty pies
> Of venison?

. . .
I have heard that on a day
Mine host's sign-board flew away,
Nobody knew whither, till
An astrologer's old quill
To a sheepskin gave the story,
Said he saw you in your glory,
Underneath a new-old sign
Sipping beverage divine,
And pledging with contented smack
The Mermaid in the Zodiac.

Wood Street runs north off Cheapside, and somewhere in this street Robert Herrick (1591–1674) was apprenticed to his uncle, a goldsmith, for ten years from the age of thirteen. This meticulous trade perhaps influenced his careful and ornamental approach to the composition of poetry:

Whenas in silks my Julia goes,
Then, then (methinks) how sweetly flows
That liquefaction of her clothes.

Next when I cast mine eyes and see
That brave Vibration each way free;
O how that glittering taketh me!

Herrick was christened in St Vedast's Church which lies west along Cheapside on the corner of Foster Lane. Rebuilt by Wren, and restored in 1962, it has a beautiful ornamented ceiling and a very fine organ. The pulpit originates from a church in Bread Street where Milton was christened. Sir John Betjeman (b. 1906) was once a churchwarden here, and has written about the bells of the City churches on a Sunday:

Sunday Silence! with every street a dead street,
    Alley and courtyard empty and cobbled mews,
Till 'tingle tang' the bell of St Mildred's Bread Street
    Summoned the sermon taster to high box pews,

And neighbouring towers and spirelets joined the ringing
    With answering echoes from heavy commercial walls
Till all were drowned as the sailing clouds went singing
    On the roaring flood of a twelve-voiced peal from Paul's.

St Paul's! The view from the north, near St Vedast's, is magnificent, filling the eye's prospect, and dominating the area in a harmonious manner which contains no threat. Inside the cathedral, as well as Donne's monument, there are memorials to Dr Johnson (north choir aisle) and Blake (crypt). John Bacon, the sculptor of Johnson's statue, wanted to depict him in contemporary dress, but this was disallowed by Sir Joshua Reynolds, who decided that a Roman toga would be more suitable. *The Times* later reported:

> The rest of the Committee yielded to Reynolds' authority, and Bacon's urgent desire was overruled in favour of what has been variously described as the figure of a retired gladiator meditating on a wasted life, and as that of St Paul with a book. . . . The result was the more unfortunate in that Johnson's own objection to the relatively mild undress of the nightcapped bust made for domestic use was well known: 'though a man for ease may wear a nightcap in his own chamber,' he said, 'he ought not to look like one who had taken physic'. What would he have said to a statue of himself, in a Cathedral too, representing him as though emerging from a bath?

The ashes of Walter de la Mare (1873–1956), who for several years was a pupil at St Paul's Cathedral Choir School, are buried in the crypt. These are lines from his poem *Fare Well*:

> Look thy last on all things lovely,
> Every hour – let no night
> Seal thy sense in deathly slumber
> Till to delight
> Thou hast paid thy utmost blessing . . .

Many years before he became Dean of St Paul's, John Donne was sentenced briefly to Fleet Prison (which stood near where Fleet Lane now turns off Farringdon Street) for making a runaway marriage with the seventeen-year-old daughter of Sir George More. At the same time he lost his job as secretary to the Lord Keeper, and it was only a long thirteen years later, when he took holy orders on the advice of James I, that his fortunes began to recover. One of the pleasures of being Dean was that of hearing his own words set to music and sung in the old cathedral. *A Hymn to God the Father*, which he wrote during a serious illness, is reported by his biographer Izaak Walton to have been set

> to a most grave and solemn tune, and to be often sung to the organ by the choristers of St Paul's, in his own hearing, especially at the evening service; and at his return from his customary devotions in that place, he did occasionally say to a friend . . . 'O, the power of church music! That harmony added to this hymn has raised the affections of my heart, and quickened my graces of zeal and gratitude; and I observe that I always return from this public duty of prayer and praise to God with an unexpressible tranquility of mind, and a willingness to leave the world.'

Crossing the fairly amenable open space of modern Paternoster Square (where lovers meet in summer, a band may play, or teams of girls contest at netball), and en route for the 'Viaduct Tavern' (126 Newgate Street) with its splendid Victorian interior, perhaps one may recall the Donne of an earlier time, when he was as much concerned with love as with death. This is the first verse of a poem called *The Rising Sun* which, though no particular place is mentioned, seems to evoke an anonymous room in the city, where two lovers try to shut away the outside world:

> Busy old fool, unruly sun,
> Why dost thou thus,
> Through windows, and through curtains call on us?
> Must to thy motions lovers' seasons run?
> Saucy pedantic wretch, go chide
> Late school-boys, and sour prentices,
> Go tell court-huntsmen, that the King will ride,
> Call country ants to harvest offices;
> Love, all alike, no season knows, nor clime,
> Nor hours, days, months, which are the rags of time.

CHAPTER 4

Covent Garden

Or to some coffee-house I stray,
For news, the manna of the day . . .

wrote Matthew Green (1696–1737) in his long poem praising the
contemplative life, *The Spleen*. He would have been too young to
see John Dryden (1631–1700), nicknamed the 'Monarch' of Will's
coffee-house, but might have seen Alexander Pope (1688–1744),
another coffee-house frequenter. Will's was in Russell Street,
east of Covent Garden (where No. 21 Russell Street and the
adjacent house in Bow Street now stand), and of all the famous
seventeenth- and eighteenth-century coffee-houses it held pride
of place. Dryden, according to Dr Johnson, 'had a particular chair
to himself, which was set by the fire in winter, and was then
called his winter chair; and was carried out for him to the balcony
in summer, and was then called his summer chair'. As a child,
Pope, crippled after the illness that stunted his growth,
persuaded friends to carry him to Will's so that he might gaze at
Dryden, and by the time he was seventeen he had become an
habitué.

Besides Will's, there was in Russell Street Tom's coffee-house
on the site of what is now No. 17, and Button's – probably at
No. 10. At one time a club used to meet at Tom's, and in a verse
describing its illustrious members (who included dukes and earls
as well as Garrick and Dr Johnson), the poet laureate William
Whitehead (1715–85) mentioned that 'Here charming Goldsmith
fluttered fresh as youth'. Button's was Joseph Addison's
favourite haunt; it was run by his wife's (the Countess of
Warwick) ex-servant Daniel Button, and Addison used to retreat
there 'whenever he suffered any vexation from the countess'. For
a period Pope used to meet him there nearly every day. During
that time Pope fell out with one of Addison's cronies, the poet

Ambrose Philips (*c.* 1675–1749). Pope had written an ironical piece – to Philips's disadvantage – on the relative merits of their pastorals, and Philips is reported to have hung up a rod at Button's 'with which he threatened to chastise Pope'. Philips was nicknamed Namby-Pamby because of his sing-song, adulatory verses.

A gossip-writer of the day said of the coffee-house clientele that 'Almost every one you meet is a polite scholar or wit. Jokes and *bons mots* are exchanged from box to box, every branch of literature is critically examined and the merit of every production of the press, or performance at the theatre, weighed and examined.' It sounds like the kind of setting every young writer dreams of finding, but in 1718 the coffee-house keepers were complaining 'that their customers are afraid when it is dark to come to their houses and shops for fear that their hats and wigs should be snitched from their heads or their swords taken from their sides, or that they may be blinded, knocked down, cut or stabbed'. There was no police force then, and besides thieves and pickpockets, one contemporary claimed that 'all the prostitutes in the kingdom had picked upon that blessed neighbourhood for general rendezvous, for here are lewd women enough to fill a mighty colony . . .'.

John Gay (1685–1732) and Jonathan Swift (1667–1745) were both frequenters of the area, and it was from Swift's suggestion to Gay that a pastoral based around Newgate prison 'might make an odd pretty sort of thing' that *The Beggar's Opera* was born (which in its turn led to Brecht's *The Threepenny Opera*). Swift was a cousin of Dryden, and when he came over from Ireland to work in London he wrote odes that caused Dryden to remark: 'Cousin Swift, you will never be a poet.' Later critics have disagreed (although Swift will always be better known for his prose) and this is an extract from his light-hearted *On Poetry: A Rhapsody* in which he instructs a young poet to publish a poem and then

Portrait of Alexander Pope by Charles Jervas, Principal Portrait Painter to King George I and II. Pope addressed an adulatory poem to Jervas after receiving painting lessons from him. Dr Johnson wrote: '[Pope's] stature was so low, that to bring him to a level common with tables, it was necessary to raise his seat. But his face was not displeasing, and his eyes were animated and vivid. . . . His legs were so slender, that he enlarged their bulk with three pairs of stockings.' (*National Portrait Gallery*)

An engraving of a late seventeenth-century coffee-house. A gossip writer said of the coffee-house clientele at the time of Addison and Pope that 'Almost every one you meet is a polite scholar or wit'. (*British Museum*)

> Be sure at *Will's* the following Day,
> Lie Snug, and hear what Criticks say.
> And if you find the general Vogue
> Pronounces you a stupid Rogue;
> Damns all your Thoughts as low and little,
> Sit still, and swallow down your Spittle.
> . . .
> Your Secret kept, your Poem sunk,
> And sent in Quires to line a Trunk;
> If still you be dispos'd to rhime,
> Go try your Hand a second Time.
> Again you fail, yet Safe's the Word,
> Take Courage, and attempt a Third.

Men bathing in the River Fleet: eighteenth-century illustration for Alexander Pope's *The Dunciad*. The quotation refers to the 'thick and thin' nature of the water, which was notoriously polluted.

F. *Hayman inv. et del.*   C. *Grignion sculp.*

Here strip my Children! here at once leap in,
Here prove who best can dash thro' thick and thin.

Dunciad, Book II.

In 1817, when Will's no longer existed, Charles Lamb (1775–1834) came to live in Russell Street with his sister Mary. He wrote to Dorothy Wordsworth:

> We are in the individual spot we like best, in all this great city. The theatres with all their noises; Covent Garden, where we are morally sure of the earliest peas and 'sparagus; Bow Street, where the thieves are examined . . .

Bow Street Police Court (erected 1879) has replaced the earlier court-house, but in 1974 the vegetable, fruit and flower markets, which were the life-blood of the area, were completely moved to Nine Elms, Battersea. The future of the empty warehouses and halls led to much controversy, but the remaining community fought hard against too much impersonal commercial development, and there is a flourishing mixture of arts and crafts activities taking root in the area, as well as a number of original shops, pubs and eating places. Gradually it is becoming one of the most interesting areas of central London for visitors who are interested in the past to wander around.

Drury Lane, at the east end of Russell Street, was named after Drury House (demolished) in which Sir Robert Drury gave John Donne and his wife free use of rooms when they were hard up. The famous Theatre Royal, Drury Lane, confusingly has its back to the Lane and is entered through its huge portico in Catherine Street, off Russell Street. It is in fact the fourth theatre to be built on the site, two having been destroyed by fire. Colley Cibber (1671–1757), actor, dramatist and poet, successfully managed the second theatre, and was also poet laureate for twenty-seven years. He probably had more attacks directed against his official poetry than any other laureate (which is quite a feat), including being named as the hero of the final version of Pope's satire against bad writing and dullness, *The Dunciad*. Cibber's annual birthday odes to George II brought forth the following epigram in the *London Magazine* for 1737:

On seeing tobacco-pipes lit with one of the Laureate's odes

While the soft song that warbles George's praise
From pipe to pipe the living flame conveys,
Critics who long have scorn'd must now admire;
For who can say his ode now wants its fire?

At the beginning of the eighteenth century Drury Lane had become a second Grub Street. Pope wrote of a hack poet living 'high in Drury Lane / Lulled by soft zephyrs through the broken pane'; and Oliver Goldsmith (*c*. 1730–74), who had himself to live on hack writing, similarly described how

There, in a lonely room, from bailiffs snug,
The Muse found Scroggins, stretch'd beneath a rug.

When the Theatre Royal was rebuilt in 1812 after its second conflagration, a competition was launched for a written prologue to mark its opening. Two brothers, Horace and James Smith (1779–1849, 1775–1839), wrote twenty-one imaginary prologues, each a parody of a leading writer, which they published as *Rejected Addresses*. The collection became immensely popular, their targets including Wordsworth, Coleridge and Byron. Byron, whose own prologue was actually used, praised it highly. When the actor David Garrick began his management of the theatre in 1747, Dr Johnson provided a prologue which contained the lines:

The stage but echoes back the public voice.
The drama's laws the drama's patrons give,
For we that live to please, must please to live.

At Nos 19–20 Bow Street there is a composite plaque commemorating several former residents, including Charles Sackville, Earl of Dorset (1638–1706) and William Wycherley (*c*. 1640–1716). Sackville was a minor poet and popular courtier, who was Nell Gwyn's lover before she took up with Charles II. Samuel Pepys classed him with the other rakes favoured at court, whom he described as 'running up and down all the night, almost naked, through the streets; and at last fighting, and being beat by the watch and clapped up all night; and the king takes their parts . . . '. However, Sackville sobered up in middle life and gave practical help to many fellow writers, including Dryden and Matthew Prior. Wycherley is primarily known for his plays (*The Country Wife*, *The Plain Dealer*), but the publication of his *Miscellany Poems* led to a friendship with Pope (then a precocious sixteen), and it is the latter who described the marriage which took place at Bow Street eleven days before Wycherley died, in order to spite his heir and settle his immediate cash debts:

He had often told me . . . that he would marry as soon as his life was despaired of. Accordingly, a few days before his death, he underwent the ceremony. . . . The old man then lay down, satisfied in the conscience of having by this one act paid his just debts, obliged a woman who (he was told) had merit, and shown an heroic resentment of the ill-usage of his next heir. Some hundred pounds which he had with the lady discharged those debts; a jointure of four hundred a year made her a recompense; and the nephew he left to comfort himself as well as he could with the miserable remains of a mortgaged estate.

Wycherley was buried in St Paul's Church, which was designed by Inigo Jones and is approached from the west, off Bedford Street. The great Tuscan portico of the church, which faces the newly-restored piazza and the redeveloped Covent Garden, should have been the main entrance, but Bishop Laud insisted the altar be placed at the east end of the church, rather than the west as Jones had intended. John Gay evokes the scene in the piazza one winter's day in the eighteenth century with this description of an impromptu football game:

> Where Covent Garden's famous temple stands,
> That boasts the work of Jones' immortal hands;
> Columns with plain magnificence appear,
> And graceful porches lead along the square:
> Here oft my course I bend, when lo! from far,
> I spy the furies of the football war:
> The 'prentice quits his shop, to join the crew,
> Increasing crowds the flying game pursue.
> Thus, as you roll the ball o'er snowy ground,
> The gath'ring globe augments with every round.
> But whither shall I run? The throng draws nigh,
> The ball now skims the street, now soars on high;
> The dext'rous glazier strong returns the bound,
> And jingling sashes on the pent-house sound.

Samuel Butler, author of *Hudibras*, is also buried at St Paul's, though it is primarily known as the 'actors' church', and contains memorials to many famous people of the theatre. Inigo Jones himself was responsible for introducing the proscenium arch and movable scenery to the English stage, and he designed the settings for numerous court masques, including some by Ben Jonson. However, the two men quarrelled, and Jonson replied to Jones's complaints with two satires entitled *An Expostulation with Inigo Jones* and *A Corollary to Inigo Marquis Would-be*. He then proceeded to ridicule him further in *A Tale of a Tub*.

There is a plaque in the church which was erected by the painter J. M. W. Turner to the memory of his parents, the family having lived in Henrietta Street, which runs between Bedford Street and Covent Garden. (The house was demolished.) Turner's great painting *Cottage destroyed by an avalanche* is an interpretation of lines from James Thomson's *Winter*:

Oft, rushing sudden from the loaded cliffs,
Mountains of snow their gathering terrors roll,
From steep to steep, loud thundering down they come,
A wintry waste in dire commotion all . . .

And Turner himself explored many of his pessimistic ideas and preoccupations in a long poem, *Fallacies of Hope*, which he used as a means of expression parallel to his painting.

Bedford Street runs north into Garrick Street, off which leads narrow Rose Street. This was the site where, on the night of 18 December 1679, Dryden was severely beaten up, supposedly by three men hired by the Earl of Rochester who had been angered by an anonymous satire upon him which he had wrongly attributed to Dryden. At the top of Rose Street is a Victorian pub, the 'Lamb and Flag', which is now sometimes used by the Writers' Guild for meetings. Garrick Street converges with the western end of Long Acre, where Dryden lived at No. 137 (house demolished) for a period. Phoenix Alley (demolished) ran off the middle of Long Acre, and was the site of a tavern kept by John Taylor (1580–1653), 'The Water Poet'. He was a Thames waterman who wrote boisterous verses which became very popular – Ben Jonson is said to have liked them. His tavern was called the 'Poet's Head', and he used his own portrait on the sign together with this inscription:

There's many a head stands for a sign;
Then, gentle reader, why not mine?

When horse-carriages began to become popular at the beginning of the seventeenth century, Taylor made an impassioned plea for the watermen, who were losing trade to the hackney coaches:

This infernal swarm of trade spillers have so overrun the
land, that we can get no living on the water . . . I pray you
look into the streets, how they are pestered with them,
especially after a mask or a play at the court, where even the
very earth quakes and trembles, the casements shatter, tatter,
and clatter, and such a confused noise is made, so that a man
can neither sleep, speak, hear, write, nor eat his dinner or
supper quiet for them.

And we tend to think of traffic as a recent menace!

Neal Street, on the north side of Long Acre, leads out of the
Covent Garden area, across Shaftesbury Avenue to St Giles's
High Street, where the church of St Giles-in-the-Fields (1733,
restored 1954) stands near the notorious Centrepoint tower block
and Denmark Street, traditional home of music publishers and
nicknamed Tin Pan Alley. The parish register records that in 1648
Milton's daughter Mary was baptized in the earlier church which
stood on the site. On 9 March 1818 a triple christening took place:
the Shelleys' children, William and Clara, and Claire Clairmont's
child, Clara Allegra, recorded as 'reputed daughter of Rt Hon.
George Gordon, Lord Byron, Peer of no fixed residence,
travelling on the continent'. Three days later they all departed for
Italy. It was after visiting Byron in Venice that Shelley wrote
Julian and Maddalo, an autobiographical account of their meeting
and discussions, which contains this description of Allegra:

And whilst I waited with this child I played;
A lovelier toy sweet Nature never made,
A serious, subtle, wild, yet gentle being,
Graceful without design and unforeseeing,
With eyes – Oh speak not of her eyes! – which seem
Twin mirrors of Italian Heaven, yet gleam
With such deep meaning, as we never see
But in the human countenance: with me
She was a special favourite: I had nursed
Her fine and feeble limbs when she came first
To this bleak world; and she yet seemed to know

John Dryden in front of the 'Lamb and Flag' pub, Rose Street, Covent Garden.
Dryden was beaten up on this site, then known as Rose Alley, by a masked gang
who wrongly thought he was responsible for ridiculing the Earl of Rochester in an
anonymous satire.

On second sight her antient playfellow,
Less changed than she was by six months or so;
For after her first shyness was worn out
We sate there, rolling billiard balls about . . .

In the north aisle of St Giles there is a monument to George Chapman (d. 1634) designed by Inigo Jones, and a tablet to Andrew Marvell (1621–78) erected by his great-nephew in 1764. Both poets were buried at the church. The inscription on Marvell's tablet extols his virtues as a member of parliament rather than a poet, reminding us that he had a reputation for incorruptibility. Although a supporter of Cromwell, he showed humane sympathy for Charles I when describing his execution in *An Horatian Ode upon Cromwell's Return from Ireland*:

He nothing common did or mean
Upon that memorable Scene;
   But with his keener Eye
   The Axe's edge did try:
Nor call'd the Gods with vulgar spight
To vindicate his helpless Right,
   But bow'd his comely Head,
   Down, as upon a Bed.

James Shirley (1596–1666), poet and playwright, was buried with his wife in St Giles's churchyard (site unknown), both having died on the same day two months after they were driven from their home near Fleet Street by the Great Fire. They were, it is reported, 'overcome with affrightments, disconsolations and other miseries occasioned by that fire and their losses'. One of Shirley's dramas ends with a dirge which had proved a popular source for tombstone quotations. Here is one of its three verses:

The glories of our blood and state,
   are shadows, not substantial things,
There is no armour against Fate,
   Death lays his icy hand on Kings,
     Scepter and Crown,
     Must tumble down,
And in the dust be equal made,
With the poor crooked sithe and spade.

St Giles-in-the-Fields, near Tottenham Court Road underground station. As its name suggests, this was once a rural part of London.

CHAPTER 5

Strand, Fleet Street, Inns of Court and Holborn

This section of the city, shaped like an inverted T, has some of London's most unexpected and secluded green spaces hidden among the Inns of Court, and also one of its busiest thoroughfares – Fleet Street, centre of the newspaper industry. Hundreds of lawyers and journalists work in the area and congregate at lunchtime and early evening in the numerous public houses; and both professions from time to time receive brickbats from the poets. Coleridge and Southey, in their joint satire *The Devil's Thoughts*, had a dig at the lawyers:

> He saw a Lawyer killing a viper
>   On a dunghill hard by his own stable;
> And the Devil smiled, for it put him in mind
>   Of Cain and his brother, Abel.

And Humbert Wolfe (1886–1940), in a contribution in *Punch*, was equally unkind to journalists:

> You cannot hope
> To bribe or twist
> Thank God! The British Journalist.
> But seeing what
> That man will do
> Unbribed, there's no occasion to.

However, while providing good targets for satire, the professions of law and journalism have always lured some of the best brains, several poets included.

Not only is this an area of contrast between bustle and calm, but also between grandeur and decay. And by starting at the western tip of the T-shape, in Craven Street (off the Strand, west of Charing Cross station), a certain amount of decay is pre-eminent. It was here that the German poet, Heinrich Heine (1797–1856), lodged for three months in 1827, commemorated by a plaque on No. 32 (now the London Airgun Centre). On 23 April he wrote to a friend: 'It is snowing outside, and there is no fire in my chimney . . . London has surpassed all my expectations as to its magnificence, but I have lost myself. Living is terribly dear here.' Years later he commented: ' . . . do not send a poet to London! The mere seriousness of everything, the colossal uniformity, the machine-like movement, the shrillness even of joy – this over-driven London oppresses fancy and rends the heart.'

Standing at the Strand end of Craven Street, one can look down, across Northumberland Avenue, at the trees bordering the Thames along the Victoria Embankment, and recall that before the embankment was built, boats would have been drawn up at the river's edge. The brothers Smith, James and Horace, chose the street as the setting for their anti-lawyer verse-pun:

In Craven-street, Strand, ten attorneys find place,
And ten dark coal-barges are moor'd at its base.
Fly Honesty, fly! seek some safer retreat;
For there's craft in the river, and craft in the street.

On the east side of the street, Craven Passage leads under the railway to Villiers Street. The great music-hall entertainers, Bud Flanagan and Chesney Allen, made these arches famous in their song *Underneath the Arches*. No. 43 Villiers Street was where Rudyard Kipling (1865–1936) lived in three rooms on the second floor from 1889 to 1891. The block has been renamed Kipling House and carries a commemorative plaque. He used to look from his desk across to Gatti's music hall, where he sometimes took 'an elderly but upright barmaid from a pub nearby' whose life story inspired his poem *'Mary, Pity Women'* from which this is taken:

Nice while it lasted, an' now it is over –
Tear out your 'eart an' good-bye to your lover!
What's the use o' grievin', when the mother that bore you
(Mary, pity women!) knew it all before you?

Kipling said that 'the smoke, the roar and the good fellowship' of

Gatti's influenced him to write the type of song in *Barrack-Room Ballads*, and the performance of Victorian music-hall songs has endured at what is now the Players' Theatre opposite Kipling House. At the bottom of the street Charing Cross Railway Bridge (paralleled by Hungerford Foot Bridge) crosses to the South Bank arts complex, and the arches formed by these have long provided mean shelter for London's tramps and homeless. D. H. Lawrence (1885–1930), when he was a young man working as a teacher in Croydon, had a compassionate eye for the dispossessed; these are extracts from his *Embankment at Night*:

> At Charing Cross, here, beneath the bridge
> Sleep in a row the outcasts,
> Packed in a line with their heads against the wall.
> Their feet in a broken ridge
> Stretched out on the way, and a lout casts
> A look as he stands on the edge of this naked stall.
> . . .
> The balls of five red toes
> As red and dirty, bare
> Young birds forsaken and left in a nest of mud –
> Newspaper sheets enclose
> Some limbs like parcels, and tear
> When the sleeper stirs or turns on the ebb of the flood –
>
> One heaped mound
> Of a woman's knees
> As she thrusts them upward under the ruffled skirt –
> And a curious dearth of sound
> In the presence of these
> Wastrels that sleep on the flagstones without any hurt.
> . . .
> On the outer pavement, slowly,
> Theatre people pass,
> Holding aloft their umbrellas that flash and are bright
> Like flowers of infernal moly
> Over nocturnal grass
> Wetly bobbing and drifting away on our sight.

John Adam Street runs eastwards from Villiers Street, a reminder that this area, known as The Adelphi, was planned by the four Scottish brothers Adam in the eighteenth century. A few

Adam houses remain, notably in Adam Street itself. Another architect, who became better known as a poet and novelist, Thomas Hardy (1840–1928), was employed in offices in Adelphi Terrace from 1862 to 1867, the period during which the Victoria Embankment and Charing Cross bridge were being built. The Adam building he worked in was demolished, replaced by the present 1938 structure of quite remarkable grandiloquence. Hardy used to find the marble Adam fireplaces 'useful to make quick sketches' on, and among the new buildings being erected in the area that he made detailed notes on was the Strand Music Hall (now demolished) with its cast-iron columns with copper foliations.

Robert Street, which runs between Adelphi Terrace and John Adam Street, has a plaque on Nos 1–3 (rebuilt) remarking that Robert Adams, John Galsworthy, James Barrie, and the poet and editor Thomas Hood (1799–1845) have all lived there. Hood, perhaps best known for his comic verses, wrote a poem about the Lord Mayor's Show, the yearly occasion when the new Lord Mayor of London is led by coach through the streets of the City preceded by a procession. It starts:

How well I remember the ninth of November
The Sky very foggy, the Sun looking groggy,
In fact, altogether pea-soup colour's weather . . .

reminding us of the days when London was not a smokeless zone and 'pea-soup' fogs were a regular November occurrence. When Hood's daughter died at birth, his friend Charles Lamb wrote *On an Infant Dying as soon as Born*, containing the lines:

Riddle of destiny, who can show
What thy short visit meant, or know
What thy errand here below?

Durham House Street, a narrow dead-end alley which runs north off John Adam Street, marks the site of Durham House, the home of the first Earl of Essex, where Sir Philip Sidney (1554–86) met Essex's daughter Penelope, the Stella of his sonnets *Astrophel and Stella*. She was forced to marry someone else, and the sonnets express his personal sadness and passion as well as being a meditation on the nature of love in general. These lines bemoan Cupid's ubiquity:

With how sad steps, O Moone, thou climbst the skies,
How silently, and with how wanne a face,
What, may it be that even in heav'nly place
That busy archer his sharpe arrowes tries?

At the end of Durham House Street is the entrance to the Arthur
Murray Dance Studio, bringing a shadow of a reminder of the
grandeur and glamour of dancing in centuries past, wistfully
recalled in Hardy's *Reminiscences of a Dancing Man*. These are two
of its verses; Almack's (later Willis's) Rooms in St James's were
the scene of exclusive assemblies and balls, and Cremorne
Gardens were on the river near World's End, Chelsea:

Who now remembers Almack's balls –
Willis's sometime named –
In those two smooth-floored upper halls
For faded ones so famed?
Where as we trod to trilling sound
The fancied phantoms stood around,
Or joined us in the maze,
Of the powdered Dears from Georgian years,
Whose dust lay in sightless sealed-up biers,
The fairest of former days.

Who now remembers gay Cremorne,
And all its jaunty jills,
And those wild whirling figures born
Of Jullien's grand quadrilles?
With hats on head and morning coats
There footed to his prancing notes
Our partner-girls and we;
And the gas-jets winked, and the lustres clinked,
And the platform throbbed as with arms enlinked
We moved to the minstrelsy.

The 'Gilbert and Sullivan' public house in John Adam Street
contains relics of the authors of the comic operas which used
to be presented at the nearby Savoy Theatre. W. S. Gilbert
(1836–1911), who supplied the words, also wrote *Bab Ballads*, a
very popular collection of humorous verse. The name Savoy,
given to the hotel, theatre, and surrounding streets, comes from
Savoy Palace which was built on the site in 1246 with gardens

A formal photograph of Thomas Hardy. 'The face seemed to betoken a weathering of infinite experiences, of communion with ghostly images of thought and imagination . . . ' (W. M. Parker). (*British Museum*)

Drawing of William Blake (left) in conversation with John Varley, by their friend John Linnel. Linnel once remarked: 'Varley believed in the reality of Blake's visions more than even Blake himself.' (*Fitzwilliam Museum, Cambridge*)

stretching down to the river. John of Gaunt became its owner, and Chaucer wrote some of his poetry there. When Wat Tyler burned the palace down, Henry VII built a chapel and hospital on the site and a heavily-restored version of that chapel survives, known as the Queen's Chapel of the Savoy (entrance in Savoy Hill). It has a memorial window to Chaucer.

On the south side of the Strand (Nos 103–4), Savoy Buildings has ceramic entrance plaques recording that Fountain Court, an alleyway, once occupied the site. William Blake (1757–1827) spent the last six years of his life in rooms on the first floor of No. 3 Fountain Court, where from his work-table he could look up and see the Thames 'like a bar of gold'. A few days before he died he said to his wife, Catherine: 'Stay! keep as you are! *you* have ever been an *angel* to me, I will draw you.' A friend reported that on the afternoon of his death

He said He was going to that Country he had all His life wished to see and expressed himself Happy hoping for Salvation through Jesus Christ – Just before he died His countenance became fair – His eyes Brighten'd and He burst out in singing of the things he saw in Heaven.

Essex Street, which turns south off the Strand near St Clement Danes Church (whose bells inspired the rhyme 'Oranges and lemons, say the bells of St Clement's'), is the site of Leicester House, Tudor home of the Earl of Leicester. Edmund Spenser was one of the household before he went to Ireland, and he met Leicester's nephew, Philip Sidney, here and together they formed the Areopagus Club with the aim of improving the standard of English poetry. Spenser stayed there again when visiting from Ireland and wrote *Prothalamion* in celebration of the double marriage of the Earl of Worcester's two daughters, which contains the famous line, 'Sweet Thames, run softly, till I end my Song'. The narrow Devereux Court leads off Essex Street and was the site of the coffee-house known as The Grecian, being kept originally by a Greek from the Levant. Addison and Goldsmith were among its patrons, and it was famous for the learned nature of the conversations that took place there. 'The Devereux' public house stands on the actual site.

A gate opposite leads into The Temple, the two Inns of Court known as the Middle Temple and the Inner Temple. In *The Prelude* Wordsworth contrasted the dirty alleyways that then surrounded the Inns of Court with the more salubrious settings inside the gates:

> Private Courts,
> Gloomy as Coffins, and unsightly Lanes
> Thrill'd by some female Vendor's scream, belike
> The very shrillest of all London Cries,
> May then entangle us awhile;
> Conducted through those labyrinths, unawares,
> To privileg'd Regions and inviolate,
> Where from their airy lodges studious Lawyers
> Look out on waters, walks, and gardens green.

The area retains an atmosphere of peace and privilege.

Shakespeare's *Twelfth Night* received its first presentation at Middle Temple Hall, attended by the Queen. The Hall was badly bombed in the Second World War, but has been rebuilt and restored. According to a scene in *Henry VI, Part I*, the white and red roses assumed as badges in the Wars of the Roses were first picked in the gardens of The Temple. Oliver Goldsmith (*c.* 1730–74) lived at Brick Court (rebuilt) from 1765 until his death and is buried in the upper part of the Temple Church graveyard.

Charles Lamb (1775–1834) was born at Crown Office Row (rebuilt) and lived there until he was twenty, his father being confidential clerk to a lawyer called Samuel Salt. There is a fountain commemorating Lamb in the Gardens – a stone figure of a boy inscribed with a quotation by him: 'Lawyers were children once.' Many writers have been members of the Inner and Middle Temples, though it was not uncommon for them to abandon their studies before being called to the Bar. William Cowper did complete his, but then never practised, being singularly unsuited to the profession of lawyer.

The Strand runs into Fleet Street just by the Wren gateway to Middle Temple Lane, No. 1 Fleet Street being Child's Bank, one of the oldest-established banks in London. (Its present building was erected in 1879, and it is now amalgamated with Williams & Glyn's Bank.) Part of its site was once the 'Devil Tavern', where Ben Jonson founded the Apollo Club whose members were not permitted to recite 'insipid' verse. A plaque commemorates the Tavern. The old bank used to stand next door, and Dryden deposited £50 there in 1679 as a reward for the identification of the hired ruffians who had beaten him up in Rose Alley (now Street). When Colley Cibber was poet laureate he used to rehearse his court odes to music at the Tavern, a fact derisively referred to by Pope in *The Dunciad*.

Engraving of St Bride's, Fleet Street by John Bowles, after it had been rebuilt by Wren: Earlier Milton had lived in St Bride's Churchyard with his first wife, but 'she found it very solitary; no company came . . . this life was irksome to her, and so she went to her parents' (John Aubrey). (*Guildhall Library*)

On the north side of Fleet Street between Chancery Lane and Fetter Lane is the church of St Dunstan in the West, where Donne was rector for the last seven years of his life (as well as being Dean of St Paul's Cathedral). In the final sermon which he preached here, when he was very ill, he said: 'When my mouth shall be filled with dust, and the worms shall feed and feed sweetly upon me, when the ambitious man shall have no satisfaction if the poorest alive tread upon him, nor the poorest receive any contentment in being made equal to princes, for they shall be equal but in dust'. His biographer, Izaak Walton, held the position of 'Scavenger, Questman and Sidesman' at the church and is commemorated by a tablet on the wall outside and a stained-glass window. The latter stands behind a large Romanian icon-screen, the church being partially used by the Romanian Orthodox Church. Thomas Campion (d. 1620) and Thomas Carew (*c.* 1598–1639) were both buried here. Carew wrote an *Elegy on the Death of Donne* containing these lines:

Here lies a King that rul'd, as he thought fit
The universal monarchy of wit;
Here lies two Flamens, and both those the best:
Apollo's first, at last the true God's priest.

Campion set some of his own poems to music, including one that begins:

There is a Garden in her face,
Where Roses and white Lillies grow;
A heav'nly paradise is that place,
Wherein all pleasant fruits doe flow.

Outside on the wall of the church is a clock made in 1671 with figures that strike the quarter hour. Cowper refers to it in his poem *Table Talk* when he is propounding that poetry should not be too refined and regular:

Give me the line that ploughs its stately course,
Like a proud swan, conquering the stream by force;
That like some cottage beauty, strikes the heart,
Quite unindebted to the tricks of art.
When labour and when dulness, club in hand,
Like the two figures at St Dunstan's stand,

Beating alternately, in measured time,
The clockwork tintinabulum of rhyme,
Exact and regular the sounds will be;
But such mere quarter-strokes are not for me.

Keeping to the north side of Fleet Street, past Fetter Lane, one comes to a series of small courts and alleys. Dr Johnson lived for eleven years in Johnson's Court – it already had that name when he moved there and is not named after him – and he spent the last years of his life in Bolt Court; both houses are now demolished. These courts lead into Gough Square which contains the actual house he lived in from 1749 to 1758, while he was preparing his Dictionary. The house is run by a Trust and contains many very interesting relics of Johnson's life. It is open to the public (10.30–4.30, Monday–Saturday) and is well worth a visit, not least to see a carefully-restored interior of a private house built *c.* 1700. Nowadays it is very clean and neat, but Johnson's biographer, Margaret Lane, reminds us that it was different in his day, especially after his wife died:

> the house in Gough Square, now more than ever
> disorganised and comfortless, began to assume that
> miscellaneous and slightly freakish character which was to
> distinguish Johnson's household for the rest of his life.
> Robert Levett was there already, dark, dusty and silent,
> attending to his back-street practice by day and at night
> available as undemanding company. . . . The anonymous
> maidservant lived her life below stairs, and . . . If any of the
> five copyists slept in the garret with the Dictionary (as indeed
> they may have done, since all Johnson could pay them was
> twenty-three shillings a week between them) they were sober
> and needy men who gave little trouble. . . . But the third
> week after the funeral saw the introduction of a new and
> surprising inmate, who for the remaining thirty years of
> Johnson's life was to be both an exasperation and a comfort.
> This was a Negro boy called Francis Barber, who at the time
> of his coming under Johnson's wing seems to have been
> about six or seven years old.

Johnson's friend Goldsmith lived for a time in Wine Office Court (which now has a house named after him), and they both used to frequent the 'Cheshire Cheese' which is in the same Court and

The 'Cheshire Cheese' pub (rebuilt 1667), 145 Fleet Street, in 1979. The Rhymers' Club, of which W. B. Yeats was a founder, met here in the 1890s, while Dr Johnson and Oliver Goldsmith were customers in the 1760s. (*Longman Picture Library*)

has its entrance at 145 Fleet Street. This very old pub was rebuilt in 1667 after the Great Fire and has been a gathering place for innumerable writers and journalists. In the 1890s the Rhymers' Club, founded by W. B. Yeats (1865–1939) and Ernest Rhys, used to meet there; its members included Lionel Johnson, Ernest Dowson, John Davidson and Richard Le Gallienne, and they would drink together and read their poems aloud. Dowson's (1867–1900) *Cynara*, from which the following verses are taken, recreates the mood of the so-called decadent Nineties – it was first read at a meeting of the Rhymers' Club:

> Last night, ah, yesternight, betwixt her lips and mine
> There fell thy shadow, Cynara! thy breath was shed
> Upon my soul between the kisses and the wine;
> And I was desolate and sick of an old passion,
>   Yea, I was desolate and bowed my head:
> I have been faithful to thee, Cynara! in my fashion.

Dr Johnson in the dining-room of his house in Gough Square, Fleet Street, in conversation with Oliver Goldsmith.

. . .

I have forgot much, Cynara! gone with the wind,
Flung roses, roses riotously with the throng,
Dancing, to put thy pale, lost lilies out of mind;
But I was desolate and sick of an old passion,
　Yea, all the time, because the dance was long:
I have been faithful to thee, Cynara! in my fashion.

Cole Porter made good use of the final line in *Always True to You*
(*In My Fashion*), one of the songs from *Kiss Me, Kate* – itself based
on Shakespeare's *The Taming of the Shrew*.

A little way up Chancery Lane from Fleet Street, on the
right-hand side, is the Public Record Office which contains the
Record Office Museum (open restricted hours). Among its
exhibits are Shakespeare's signature and will, Dr Johnson's will,
and some memorials of Shelley. Opposite lies Carey Street,
whose name became synonymous with insolvency when the
Bankruptcy Court was erected there. Serle Street leads off to the
north, and was once the site of Serle's Coffee House, where,
among others, the physician and minor poet Mark Akenside
(1721–70) used to preside. He was lamed in an accident involving
his father's butcher's cleaver, but this did not help him feel
sympathy for his patients, and when he became an eminent
doctor 'He would order the hospital servants on his visiting days,
to precede him with brooms to clear the way, and prevent the
patients from too nearly approaching him.'

Serle Street leads to Lincoln's Inn Fields, the largest square in
central London and containing some very fine trees. Lincoln's
Inn lies to the east, and its members have included John Donne
and the prime minister Benjamin Disraeli – who began his literary
career as a poet before becoming more successful as a novelist.
Donne was made Master of the Revels for festivities held at the
Inn during February 1593. Nowadays the square is a place of
recreation and refuge, but in John Gay's time it was a
headquarters of beggars by day and robbers at night:

Where Lincoln's Inn's wide space is railed around,
Cross not with venturous step; there oft is found
The lurking thief, who, while the daylight shone,
Made the walls echo with his begging tone.
That crutch, which late compassion mov'd, shall wound
Thy bleeding head, and fell thee to the ground.

Though thou art tempted by the linkman's call,
Yet trust him not along the lonely wall;
In the midway he'll quench the flaming brand
And share the booty with the pilfering band.

Linkmen used to carry flaming torches made of tow and pitch in order to light people along the dark streets.

Leaving Lincoln's Inn Fields by Remnant Street one comes into Kingsway, opposite Great Queen Street. It was in the latter that William Blake was apprenticed at the age of fourteen to the engraver James Basire (at No. 31, now rebuilt). Basire was not Blake's father's first choice, for he had originally taken his son to a popular artist called William Ryland. But the young Blake had said: 'Father, I do not like the man's look; he looks as if he would live to be hanged.' So Basire was selected instead. And twelve years later Ryland was hanged for forgery. During the time Blake was with Basire, Goldsmith called at the workshop and Blake envied his finely shaped head. He also admired his work and later remarked that 'Such Men as Goldsmith ought not to have been Acquainted with such Men as Reynolds.' Blake's disapproval of Sir Joshua Reynolds, President of the Royal Academy, probably dated from the time he recommended Blake to work 'with less extravagance and more simplicity, and to correct his drawing' after Blake became a student at the Academy. There is an interesting artists' colourmen's shop at No 22 Great Queen Street, established in 1855, which sells old-fashioned jars and packets of colours, giving a reminder of how artists' materials looked nearer to Blake's time. It also stocks quill pens, and Blake mentions another kind of pen made from natural resources in his introductory poem to *Songs of Innocence*. These are the last verses; a child is addressing the author, who is in the guise of a piper:

'Piper, sit thee down and write
In a book, that all may read.'
So he vanish'd from my sight,
And I pluck'd a hollow reed.

And I made a rural pen,
And I stain'd the water clear,
And I wrote my happy songs
Every child may joy to hear.

When Charles Lamb's family had to move from The Temple, they went into lodgings in Little Queen Street. The street no longer exists, but it used to be on the site of Holy Trinity Church, a little further north up Kingsway past Great Queen Street. This was twenty years after Blake's apprenticeship, and as far as we know the two men never met, though Lamb was an admirer of both his paintings and his poems. When he heard someone recite *The Tyger*, he said that he 'must look on Blake as one of the most extraordinary persons of the age'. It was at Little Queen Street that a tragedy occurred within the Lamb family. They were in poor circumstances: Mr Lamb was elderly and could no longer work; Mrs Lamb was ill, and sometimes mentally disturbed; and Charles's sister, Mary, had to assume nursing and household duties, as well as earn money from needlework. On 27 September 1796, 21-year-old Charles wrote to his friend S. T. Coleridge:

> some of my friends, or the public papers, by this time may
> have informed you of the terrible calamities that have fallen
> on our family. I will only give you the outlines: My poor,
> dear, dearest sister, in a fit of insanity, has been the death of
> our own mother. I was at hand only time enough to snatch
> the knife out of her grasp. She is at present in a madhouse,
> from whence I fear she must be moved to a hospital. God has
> preserved me to my senses, – I eat and drink and sleep, and
> have my judgment, I believe, very sound. My poor father
> was slightly wounded, and I am left to take care of him and
> my aunt.

Charles resumed responsibility for Mary, and she was released from hospital and shared his various homes until his death.

At the top of Kingsway, High Holborn leads eastwards to Fulwood Place, which turns left into Gray's Inn. The garden is open to the public only at restricted times, but one can look through the fine iron gates to the croquet lawn and ancient catalpa trees. At least one of the latter is supposed to have been grown from a cutting brought back from America by Ralegh. The gardens were designed by Francis Bacon (1561–1626), the Inn's most distinguished member, and he and Ralegh used to stroll there arm in arm. It became a fashionable place for meeting, and Lamb called the gardens 'the best of any in the Inns of Court, my beloved Temple not forgotten'. Members of Gray's Inn have included Thomas Campion, whose songs were used in a masque produced there; James Shirley, who wrote the text for another masque; and Southey, who abandoned his law studies when he found them a 'laborious indulgence'. The buildings of Gray's Inn were heavily damaged by bombs, but are now restored, including The Hall on the north side of South Square, where Shakespeare's *The Comedy of Errors* was first performed.

Crossing the juncture of Gray's Inn Road and Holborn, the next turning on the left is Brooke Street. It was here that Thomas Chatterton (1752–70) poisoned himself with arsenic in an attic room at the age of seventeen. (The house, now demolished, was on the site of No. 39.) Chatterton came from a poor Bristol family, and travelled to London to seek his fortune after creating an impression with precocious poems written in convincing medieval style and purporting to be by one Thomas Rowley, a fifteenth-century priest. Chatterton's pride, combined with the prevailing social snobbery of the day, prevented him from making a living, though he did manage to sell an operetta which was performed at the Marylebone pleasure gardens. With the fee for this, he was able to send gifts to his mother and sister, and told them how he went to the coffee-houses: 'I am quite familiar at the Chapter Coffee House, and know all the geniuses there. A character is now unnecessary; an author carries his genius in his pen.' He lasted only four months in London; his biographer John Davis described his end at Brooke Street, where he lodged with Mrs Angel, a sack-maker:

Of his extreme indigence there is positive testimony. Mrs Angel remembers that for two days, when he did not absent himself from his room, he went without food. . . . Mr Cross, an apothecary in Brooke Street, bore evidence that while Chatterton lived with Mrs Angel, he frequently called at the shop, and was repeatedly pressed by Mr Cross to dine or sup with him, but always in vain. One evening, however, hunger so far prevailed over his pride as to tempt him to partake of a barrel of oysters, when he was observed to eat most voraciously. . . . Pressed hard by indigence and its companions, gloom and despondency, the mind of Chatterton became disordered, and on the night of the 24th August, 1770, he swallowed a large dose of poison, which caused his death. . . . The inquest of the jury was brought in insanity, and the body of Chatterton was put into a shell, and

87

The Death of Chatterton, painting by Henry Wallis. Thomas Chatterton poisoned himself in 1770 at the age of seventeen. In 1856 Wallis 'searched out the very same attic in Gray's Inn in which the poet had killed himself, and used the wan light of dawn to shed lustre on this purple-trousered cadaver, its flesh lily-livid . . . ' (Timothy Hilton). (*Tate Gallery*)

carried unwept, unheeded, and unowned to the burying-ground of the workhouse in Shoe Lane.

That cemetery no longer exists.

At the corner of a small square at the top of Brooke Street is the church of St Alban the Martyr. It looks rather neglected now, but in the nineteenth century it was a fashionable High Church, known for its ritual, and together with other Oxford undergraduates Gerard Manley Hopkins sometimes attended its services before he became a Roman Catholic. Returning to Holborn, on the south-east corner of Holborn Circus is St Andrew's Church, designed by Wren and restored after being ruined by bombs in 1940. Disraeli was baptized there when he was twelve, his father having decided that they should leave the Jewish faith because it was too narrow. Charles and Mary Lamb attended the marriage of the essayist William Hazlitt there, Lamb reporting that 'I was at Hazlitt's marriage, and had liked to have been turned out several times during the ceremony. Anything awful makes me laugh.'

Lamb once likened the quality of the dirge in John Webster's (*c.* 1580–*c.* 1625) *The White Devil* ('Call for the robin redbreast, and the wren, / Since o'er shady groves they hover'), to Shakespeare's 'Full fathom five they father lies; / Of his bones are coral made', saying: 'As that is of the water, watery, so this is of the earth, earthy.' And a good deal of that earthiness probably came from Webster's experience when living in the parish of St Sepulchre at the eastern end of Holborn Viaduct. The Old Bailey now stands opposite the church, but in Webster's time it was Newgate prison, and in 1605 a benefactor gave £50 for the parish clerk to toll the great bell of St Sepulchre on the eve of executions at Tyburn, and also to stand at midnight outside the condemned cell giving 'twelve solemn tolls' on a handbell (still in the church) and exhorting prisoners to repent. This custom appears in *The Duchess of Malfi* when Bosola says:

> I am the common bellman
> That usually is sent to condemn'd persons
> The night before they suffer

just before the Duchess is strangled. Her death speech is one of Webster's best-known passages:

> What would it pleasure me, to have my throat cut
> With diamonds? or to be smothered
> With cassia? or to be shot to death with pearls?
> I know death hath ten thousand several doors
> For men to take their exits: and 'tis found
> They go on such strange geometrical hinges,
> You may open them both ways . . .

The journey of condemned men from Newgate to Tyburn (now Marble Arch) would have had special significance for Webster inasmuch as his father, a prosperous cartwright, probably supplied the transport for their journey. As T. S. Eliot remarked in *Whispers of Immortality*: 'Webster was much possessed by death / And saw the skull beneath the skin.' Even in his dedication of *The Duchess of Malfi* to Baron Berkeley, the grave seemed to be uppermost in his mind:

> I am confident this work is not unworthy your Honour's
> perusal for by such poems as this, poets have kissed the

hands of great princes, and drawn their gentle eyes to look down upon their sheets of paper, when the poets themselves were bound up in their winding-sheets. The like courtesy from your Lordship, shall make you live in your grave, and laurel spring out of it; when the ignorant scorners of the Muses (that like worms in libraries seem to live only to destroy learning) shall wither, neglected and forgotten.

CHAPTER 6

Hampstead and Highgate

Londoners tend to divide into those who love Hampstead, and those who feel that anywhere north of Hyde Park is alien. Leigh Hunt was one of the former:

> A steeple issuing from a leafy rise,
> With balmy fields in front, and sloping green,
> Dear Hampstead, is thy southern face serene,
> Silently smiling on approaching eyes.
> Within, thine ever-shifting looks surprise,
> Streets, hills, and dells, trees overhead now seen,
> Now down below, with smoking roofs between –
> A village revelling in varieties.

And Blake was one of the latter. Here he is writing to a Hampstead friend explaining why he cannot visit him:

> I believe my Constitution to be a good one, but it has many peculiarities that no one but myself can know. When I was young, Hampstead, Highgate, Hornsea, Muswell Hill, and even Islington and all places North of London, always laid me up the day after, and sometimes two or three days. . . . Sir Francis Bacon would say, it is want of discipline in Mountainous Places. Sir Francis Bacon is a Liar. No discipline will turn one Man into another, even in the least particle . . .

Whatever each visitor's final verdict, Hampstead and Highgate provide a relaxed contrast to central London, while the Heath which lies between them is a fine place for walking and has extensive views over the city. (It could not exactly be described as a 'Mountainous Place', though it is the highest point in London; and old Hampstead is still 'A village revelling in varieties.') The quickest way to get there is by underground, but in order to take in some associations in the NW1 district, we will follow a road route which begins, somewhat arbitrarily, at 116 Lisson Grove (which runs north off Marylebone Road, west of Baker Street), once the home of the painter Benjamin Haydon (there is a plaque).

In 1817 Haydon held a dinner party in order that his young friend John Keats, then twenty-three, might fulfil his wish to meet William Wordsworth who was down in London on a visit. Haydon kept lengthy diaries, and this is an abbreviated version of his account of the evening. The two other invited guests were Charles Lamb and Thomas Monkhouse – a friend of Keats.

On December 28th the immortal dinner came off in my painting-room. . . . Wordsworth was in fine cue, and we had a glorious set-to – on Homer, Shakespeare, Milton, and Virgil. Lamb got exceedingly merry and exquisitely witty; and his fun in the midst of Wordsworth's solemn intonations of oratory was like the sarcasm and wit of the fool in the intervals of Lear's passion. . . . 'Now,' said Lamb, 'you old Lake poet, you rascally poet, why do you call Voltaire dull?' We all defended Wordsworth, and affirmed there was a state of mind when Voltaire would be dull. 'Well,' said Lamb, 'here's to Voltaire – the Messiah of the French nation, and a very proper one too.'

. . . In the morning of this delightful day, a gentleman, a perfect stranger, had called on me. He said he knew my friends, had an enthusiasm for Wordsworth, and begged I would procure him the happiness of an introduction. He told me he was a comptroller of stamps, and often had correspondence with the poet [Wordsworth was Distributor of Stamps for Westmorland]. I thought it a liberty; but still, as he seemed a gentleman, I told him he might come.

When we retired to tea we found the comptroller. In introducing him to Wordsworth I forgot to say who he was. After a little time the comptroller looked down, looked up, and said to Wordsworth: 'Don't you think, sir, Milton was a great genius?' Keats looked at me, Wordsworth looked at the comptroller, Lamb who was dozing by the fire turned round and said: 'Pray, sir, did you say Milton was a great genius?' 'No, sir; I asked Mr Wordsworth if he were not.' 'Oh,' said Lamb, 'then you are a silly fellow.' 'Charles! my dear

Charles!' said Wordsworth; but Lamb, perfectly innocent of the confusion he had created, was off again by the fire.

. . . The man in office, finding Wordsworth did not know who he was, said in spasmodic and half-chuckling anticipation of assured victory: 'I have had the honour of some correspondence with you, Mr Wordsworth.' 'With me, sir?' said Wordsworth, 'not that I remember.' 'Don't you, sir? I am the comptroller of stamps.' There was a dead silence, the comptroller evidently thinking that was enough. While we were waiting for Wordsworth's reply, Lamb sung out:

'Hey diddle diddle
The cat and the fiddle.'

'My dear Charles!' said Wordsworth.

'Diddle diddle dumpling, my son John,'
chaunted Lamb.

Haydon insists, despite everything, that 'It was indeed an immortal evening', and that 'in my life I never passed a more delightful time'. Leigh Hunt also lived in Lisson Grove (No. 15 – demolished) at that period, and ten months before Haydon's dinner party he held one at which Keats had again been present, and also Shelley. Hunt decided they should have a competition to see who could write the best sonnet on the subject of the Nile, and on the whole it was his that proved to be the most successful.

Regent's Park is a short distance east of Lisson Grove, and it was here that Edward Lear (1812–88) began his career as a draughtsman for the Zoological Society at the age of nineteen, and soon published a volume of coloured plates of the parrot family. When later he made up verses (especially limericks) to amuse the grandchildren of the Earl of Derby, he often used animals and birds (both real and imaginary) as his subject-matter. 'The Owl and the Pussy-Cat went to sea / In a beautiful pea-green boat' is the opening of one of his best-known *Nonsense Songs*. Across Prince Albert Road, north of Regent's Park, is Primrose Hill, one of the places transformed in this image from Blake's visionary poem *Jerusalem*;

The fields from Islington to Marylebone,
    To Primrose Hill and Saint John's Wood,
Were builded over with pillars of gold;
    And there Jerusalem's pillars stood.

Walter Thornbury tells how the poets of the nineteenth century eulogized Primrose Hill (which is now a favourite, but unglamorous, vantage point for Londoners seeking fresh air and a view);

> With a certain class of poets, akin to those of the 'Lake' School, it became the fashion to exalt the London suburbs as paragons of beauty. The Alps were nothing to Primrose Hill, and the elms which then crowned its summit were as the cedars of Lebanon to the ready writer.

By the mid-twentieth century, it was not easy to find release in poetical catalogues of beauty-by-comparison. Sylvia Plath (1932–63) walked on Primrose Hill with her two children in the cold winter of 1962–63 and, writes Al Alvarez in *The Savage God*, 'each trivial event became the occasion for poetry: a cut finger, a fever, a bruise'. She also noticed, in her poem *Child*, that a child's 'clear eye is the one absolutely beautiful thing' and wanted 'to fill it with colour and ducks'. In December 1962 she had moved into the top two floors of 23 Fitzroy Road – which runs off Regent's Park Road on the east side of Primrose Hill. She was attracted to the house because Yeats had lived there as a child (there is a plaque). Alvarez describes her flat:

> The children were already in bed upstairs and the flat was silent. It was newly painted, white and chill. There were, as I remember, no curtains up yet and the night pressed in coldly on the windows. She had deliberately kept the place bare: rush matting on the floor, a few books, bits of Victoriana and cloudy blue glass on the shelves, a couple of small Leonard Baskin woodcuts. It was rather beautiful, in its chaste, stripped-down way, but cold, very cold, and the oddments of flimsy Christmas decoration made it seem doubly forlorn, each seeming to repeat that she and the children would be alone over Christmas.

She died two months later. During the previous summer she had visited Yeats's Tower in Ballylee and had written to a friend that it was 'the most beautiful and peaceful place in the world'. She had

23 Fitzroy Road, NW1. W. B. Yeats's family lived here when he was a child, and it was the last home of Sylvia Plath.

Primrose Hill.

perhaps hoped to find peace in his childhood home. For Yeats himself, it had been the school holidays in Sligo with his grandparents that had been infinitely preferable to the term-time grey of Camden Town. This longing for Ireland was first expressed to his own satisfaction in the poem which begins 'I will arise and go now, and go to Innisfree.' He had developed in his teens a wish to live, in imitation of Thoreau, on the island of Innisfree in Lough Gill, and he was reminded of this wish one day by a little fountain in a Fleet Street shop window whose running water recalled the sound of the lake. His vision of 'Nine bean-rows' and 'a hive for the honey-bee' in a place where 'peace comes dropping slow, / Dropping from the veils of the morning' has been shared by many others who, like him, stop for a bewildered moment 'on the roadway, or on the pavements gray'.

Fitzroy Road leads into Gloucester Avenue, which runs up to Chalk Farm, a busy junction by the Round House – once an engine shed, now an arts centre. In 1806, however, Chalk Farm was rural and rather remote from central London, and therefore convenient for clandestine duels. Authors have always felt strongly about hostile reviews, and when the Irish poet and song writer Thomas Moore (1779–1852) was condemned by Francis Jeffrey in the *Edinburgh Review* for writing amorous odes that had 'an amoral tendency', Moore challenged him to a duel. This is part of Moore's diary entry describing the somewhat farcical occasion:

> I must have slept pretty well; for Hume, I remember, had to wake me in the morning; and the chaise being in readiness, we set off for Chalk Farm. Hume had also taken the precaution of providing a surgeon to be within call. On reaching the ground we found Jeffrey and Horner already arrived. . . . And then was it that, for the first time, my excellent friend Jeffrey and I met face to face. . . . It was agreed that the spot where we found them which was screened on one side by large trees, would be as good for our purpose as any we could select; and Horner . . . retired with Hume behind the trees, for the purpose of loading the pistols, leaving Jeffrey and myself together. We, of course, had bowed to each other at meeting; but the first words I recollect to have passed between us was Jeffrey's saying, on our being left together 'What a beautiful morning it is!' – 'Yes,' I answered with a slight smile, 'a morning made for

better purposes'; to which his only response was a sort of assenting sigh. . . . Our two friends, issuing from behind the trees, placed us at our respective posts, and put the pistols in our hands. They then retired to a little distance; the pistols were on both sides raised, and we waited for the signal to fire, when some police officers, whose approach none of us had noticed, and who were within a second of being too late, rushed out from a hedge behind Jeffrey; and one of them striking at Jeffrey's pistol with his staff, knocked it to some distance into the field, while another running over to me, took possession also of mine. We were then replaced in our respective carriages, and conveyed crestfallen to Bow Street.

It was discovered that Jeffrey's gun was not even loaded, and the two men became cordial friends. Byron, a close friend of Moore, alluded to the incident in *English Bards and Scotch Reviewers*, the satire he wrote in revenge for an anonymous review attacking his first book, which he thought (wrongly) had been written by Jeffrey.

Continuing north from Chalk Farm up Haverstock Hill, there is a pub on the left-hand side called the 'Sir Richard Steele' which is built near the site of the cottage Steele moved to in 1712 'to escape the attention of his creditors'. The 'Load of Hay' pub on the opposite side of the road was rebuilt in 1863 on the site of the old coaching inn where Addison used to alight when he came to visit Steele. Further up Haverstock Hill a right-hand turn into Pond Street, and a left-hand one into South End Grove (over South End Green), leads to Keats Grove, where Keats House is open to the public (Monday–Saturday 10–6, Sunday 2–5). This is a pair of semi-detached houses built in 1815 for two friends, Charles Wentworth Dilke and Charles Armitage Brown, and originally named Wentworth Place. Keats (1795–1821) was friendly with both of them, and when his brother Tom died from consumption and his own health was failing, Brown invited him to come and live at Wentworth Place. Dilke had by then moved out, and his house was let to Mrs Brawne, a widow with three children. Keats fell in love with her elder daughter, Fanny, then nineteen. It was during that summer of 1819 that he wrote *Ode to a Nightingale* while sitting under an ancient plum tree in the garden. These are three stanzas from the poem:

I cannot see what flowers are at my feet,
    Nor what soft incense hangs upon the boughs,
But, in embalmèd darkness, guess each sweet
    Wherewith the seasonable month endows
The grass, the thicket, and the fruit-tree wild;
    White hawthorn, and the pastoral eglantine;
        Fast fading violets cover'd up in leaves;
            And mid-May's eldest child,
        The coming musk-rose, full of dewy wine,
            The murmurous haunt of flies on summer eves.

Darkling I listen; and, for many a time
    I have been half in love with easeful Death,
Call'd him soft names in many a musèd rhyme,
    To take into the air my quiet breath;
Now more than ever seems it rich to die,
    To cease upon the midnight with no pain,
        While thou art pouring forth thy soul abroad
            In such an ecstasy!
        Still wouldst thou sing, and I have ears in vain –
            To thy high requiem become a sod.

Thou wast not born for death, immortal Bird!
    No hungry generations tread thee down;
The voice I hear this passing night was heard
    In ancient days by emperor and clown:
Perhaps the self-same song that found a path
    Through the sad heart of Ruth, when, sick for home,
        She stood in tears amid the alien corn;
            The same that oft-times hath
        Charm'd magic casements, opening on the foam
            Of perilous seas, in faery lands forlorn.

In the following February Keats developed a severe chill and coughed a drop of blood on to the sheet of his bed. Charles Brown reports what happened:

> I heard him say, 'That is blood from my mouth.' I went towards him; he was examining a single drop upon the sheet. 'Bring me a candle, Brown, and let me see this blood.' After regarding it steadfastly, he looked up in my face with a calmness of countenance I can never forget and said, 'I know the colour of that blood – it is arterial blood – I cannot be deceived in that colour – that drop of blood is my death-warrant – I must die.'

The painter Haydon came to visit him and noted 'The white curtains, the white sheets, the white shirt, and the white skin . . . all contrasted with the bright hectic flush on his cheek.' Keats did however make a slow recovery, and when Brown left London for a while he went to live in lodgings on his own; but he fell ill again, and Leigh Hunt took him to live with his family. One day Hunt inadvertently opened one of Fanny's letters, which caused a misunderstanding, and Keats returned to Wentworth Place, this time to live with the Brawnes. Doctors advised him he must winter in Italy, and he left Hampstead in September 1820, to die in Rome on 23 February 1821. Keats House has been restored and is kept as near as possible as it was when Keats knew it, and has many fascinating personal and literary relics. It was rescued from demolition in 1921 by public subscription – largely from the United States. In the public library next door is a room containing the Keats Memorial Library, with over 5,000 volumes including famous and rare editions.

Keats House, Wentworth Place, Keats Grove, Hampstead.
(*Longman Picture Library*)

The west end of Keats Grove runs into the attractive Downshire Hill, where the Scottish poet Edwin Muir (1887–1959) lived with his wife Willa Anderson at No. 7 from 1932 to 1935. In *Autobiography* Muir recounts that Hampstead then 'was filled with writing people and haunted by young poets despairing over the poor and the world, but despairing together, in a sad but comforting communion'. He and his wife translated Kafka into English and 'At one stage Kafka's stories continued themselves in our dreams, unfolding into slow serpentine nightmares, immovably reasonable.' *The Dictionary of National Biography* ends its description of his character and appearance with the somewhat enigmatic statement: 'He spoke in a soft lilting voice and sang almost in tune.'

Downshire Hill leads up to East Heath Road (where John Middleton Murry and Katherine Mansfield lived at No. 17 after their marriage) which runs along the edge of the Heath and meets Well Walk. Keats had lodgings (demolished) in Well Walk which he shared with his brother Tom until the latter's death. There was a seat in the Walk with a view towards the Heath which became known as Keats's Bench. John Masefield lived at No. 14 Well Walk from 1913 to 1916, and the painter John Constable lived at No. 40. There is a story that Blake, on a visit to Hampstead (despite his trepidation about north London), met Constable and saw a drawing of fir trees on Hampstead Heath in his sketch-book. 'Why,' exclaimed Blake, 'this is not drawing, but inspiration.' 'I meant it for drawing,' replied down-to-earth Constable.

Returning to East Heath Road, going left out of Well Walk, a right-hand turning opposite Squires Mount leads down a cul-de-sac to the Vale of Health. The present group of houses has a slightly abandoned air, but when Leigh Hunt lived there from 1816 to 1817 his cottage (demolished) was described by a local inhabitant as 'picturesque, with its pretty balcony environed with creepers, and a tall *arbor vitae* almost overtopping its roof' and the area generally was considered 'classic ground'. Shelley stayed here with Hunt during the traumatic time after his first wife Harriet (from whom he was separated) had committed suicide in the Serpentine in Hyde Park. Hunt showed him immense kindness, and a few weeks later Shelley returned accompanied by Mary Godwin, with whom he had been living for some time and had recently married. Richard Holmes, in his biography of Shelley, writes:

There were many other acquaintances who came to Hunt's fireside, to drink tea, or eat supper, or pass musical evenings surrounded by the literary busts by Shout, the pots of trailing flowers, the elegant engravings, the piles of books and galley proofs, the comfortably battered chairs and settees, and the charming suite of female cousins.

Keats and Haydon were both invited to dinner to meet Shelley, and Haydon found himself severely criticized for his Christian views:

> I went a little after the time, and seated myself in the place kept for me at table right opposite Shelley himself, as I was told after, for I did not know what hectic, spare, weakly, yet intellectual-looking creature it was carving a bit of broccoli or cabbage on his plate, as if it had been the substantial wing of a chicken. Hunt and his wife and her sister, Keats, Horace Smith and myself made up the party. In a few minutes Shelley opened the conversation by saying in a most feminine and gentle voice, 'As to that detestable religion, the Christian . . . '. I looked astounded, but casting a glance round the table, easily saw by Hunt's expression of ecstasy and the women's simper, I was to be set at that evening . . .

Keats also had reservations about Shelley, but the Hunt family loved him. Their eldest son, Thornton, then eleven, remembered expeditions on the Heath with Shelley, and sailing paper boats with him on the Vale of Health pond. Not that these walks were always serene:

> I can remember well one day when we were both for some long time engaged in gambols, broken off by my terror at his screwing up his long and curling hair into a horn, and approaching me with rampant paws and frightful gestures as some imaginative monster . . .

It was after spending a night in Hunt's cottage that Keats wrote *Sleep and Poetry*, a conversation-poem which contains this wish – which was not to be fulfilled:

> O for ten years, that I may overwhelm
> Myself in poesy; so I may do the deed
> That my own soul has to itself decreed.

In 1912 the Indian poet, Rabindranath Tagore (1861–1941) stayed at 3 Villas on the Heath, Vale of Health (there is a plaque), and published *Gitanjali* (*Song Offerings*), a collection of poems that won the Nobel Prize. There is also a plaque at 1 Byron Villas, where D. H. Lawrence stayed in 1915, the year after he had married Frieda. His novel *The Rainbow* was published that year and then suppressed as obscene, and he said bitterly, 'It is the end of my writing for England', and tried to make plans to emigrate to America. Thirteen years later he was again the victim of censorship when an exhibition of his paintings in London was suppressed because 'the authorities feared for public morals because he painted pubic hair on his nudes'. On that occasion he expressed his contempt in a comic poem, *Innocent England*, from which this is taken:

> Oh what a pity, Oh! don't you agree
> that figs aren't found in the land of the free!
>
> Fig-trees don't grow in my native land;
> there's never a fig-leaf near at hand
>
> when you want one; so I did without;
> and that is what the row's about.
>
> Virginal, pure policemen came
> and hid their faces for very shame,
>
> while they carried the shameless things away
> to gaol, to be hid from the light of day.
>
> And Mr Mead, that old, old lily
> said: 'Gross! coarse! hideous!' – and I, like a silly,
>
> thought he meant the faces of the police-court officials,
> and how right he was, and I signed my initials
>
> to confirm what he said; but alas, he meant
> my pictures, and on the proceedings went.

Spaniards Road, which crosses the Heath just past the Vale of Health, has a famous public house at either end, both of which have been, and still are, frequented by poets. At the south end, by the junction with North End Way, is 'Jack Straw's Castle',

D. H. Lawrence by Byron Villas, Vale of Health, Hampstead, where he and Frieda lodged in 1915.

which looks rather like a wooden Mississippi paddle-steamer, and at the north end, near Kenwood House, is the 'Spaniards', which was used by Leigh Hunt and his friends. Back in the main part of the village, at the bottom of Hampstead Grove (which runs parallel to Heath Street, merging with it at North End Way) and facing down Hollybush Hill, is Bolton House, one of four redbrick houses. Joanna Baillie (1762–1851), the Scottish poet and dramatist, lived here from 1806 until her death. She and her sister (who lived to be 101) led quiet lives and were well liked by several of the leading writers of the day. Wordsworth said: 'If I had to present to a foreigner any one as a model of an English gentlewoman, it would be Joanna Baillie.' She wrote this description of the view from the Heath:

It is a goodly sight through the clear air,
From Hampstead's healthy height, to see at once
England's vast capital in fair expanse –
Towers, belfries, lengthen'd streets, and structures fair,
St Paul's high dome amidst the vassal bands
Of neighbouring spires a regal chieftain stands;
And over fields of ridgy roofs appear,
With distance softly tinted, side by side
In kindred grace, like twain of sisters dear,
The Towers of Westminster, her Abbey's pride.

West of Holly Hill is the Oak Hill area (Oak Hill Way, Oak Hill Park), where Gerard Manley Hopkins (1844–89) lived as a child (exact site unidentified). The neighbourhood was then surrounded by woods and fields, and a Scottish student who lodged in the vicinity in the 1880s mentioned 'the classic arcadian calm of Oak Village, its green umbrageous nooks and its breezy atmosphere redolent of culture and the breath of the marigold . . . '. Hopkins used to enjoy climbing the tall trees in his garden, and when he was eighteen started a poem called *A Windy Day in Summer* which begins:

The vex'd elm-heads are pale with the view
Of a mastering heaven utterly blue . . .

The 'Spaniards Inn', Hampstead.

Long after he had become a Jesuit priest, Hopkins heard that his parents had decided to retire to Surrey, and wrote to his mother: 'It seemed like death at first to leave Hampstead.' During his childhood, his father was churchwarden of St John's, the Hampstead Parish Church, a short walk from Oak Hill in Church Row (near the junctions with Frognal Gardens and Holly Walk), where all the Hopkins family worshipped. It is a Georgian church, with an airy, elegant interior, and has memorials to Keats (a marble bust erected in 1894 by American admirers) and Joanna Baillie (a tablet; her grave is in the churchyard). John Constable is also buried there.

Hampstead is separated from Highgate by the Heath, and Highgate School, which Hopkins attended as a boarder from 1854 to 1862, is at the meeting point of Hampstead Lane and Highgate High Street. Returning to school after walks across the Heath on dark evenings, one of Hopkins's friends used to enjoy frightening his companions with macabre stories, one of which, called *Prometheus*, was copied out and illustrated by Hopkins. There is a story that, after an argument about how long seamen could endure without fresh water, Hopkins once wagered sixpence against ten shillings that he could survive without liquids for a given number of days. Towards the end of the experiment his tongue had turned quite black, and the headmaster found out and put an end to the wager. He was a traditionally Victorian headmaster, a one-time Lecturer in Divinity who, Hopkins once reported, 'blazed into me with his riding-whip' after Hopkins had been provoked to cheek him 'wildly'. When he was fifteen, Hopkins won the school poetry prize with *The Escorial*. Elgin House, in which he boarded – and of which he was reputed to be 'cock of the walk' – is no longer a part of the school, which has been much expanded and altered.

No. 17 North Road, which leads north off Highgate High Street near the school, was the home of A. E. Housman (1859–1936) from 1886 to 1905 (there is a plaque). He was Professor of Latin at University College, London, during part of this time, and wrote of his work translating and editing Latin poets:

A textual critic, engaged upon his business, is not at all like Newton investigating the motions of the planets: he is much more like a dog hunting for fleas. If a dog hunted for fleas on mathematical principles, he would never catch a flea, except by accident.

108

Gerard Manley Hopkins, aged twelve, in fancy dress. 'I remember a pale young boy, very light and active, with a very meditative and intellectual face' (Canon Richard Dixon).

17 North Grove, Highgate, where A. E. Housman lived for nineteen years and wrote *A Shropshire Lad*. (*Longman Picture Library*)

Housman had grown up in Worcestershire, but 'I had a sentimental feeling for Shropshire because its hills were our western horizon' and during his first years in Highgate he wrote the collection of poems called *A Shropshire Lad*. This is taken from it:

> Into my heart an air that kills
>   From yon far country blows:
> What are those blue remembered hills,
>   What spires, what farms are those?
>
> That is the land of lost content,
>   I see it shining plain,
> The happy highways where I went
>   And cannot come again.

When his Highgate landlady moved to Pinner, Housman, who lived alone, went too. Later, when he was given a professorship at Cambridge, his landlady is reported to have said that though sorry to lose him, she hoped that by living in a college he 'would be taken out of himself, shaken up, and made to chatter like the rest of the world . . . '.

Leading off Highgate High Street, opposite North Grove, is The Grove, where Samuel Taylor Coleridge (1772–1834) lived at No. 3 for the last eighteen years of his life (there is a plaque) in the house of James and Ann Gillman. Gillman, who was a surgeon, was asked by a doctor whether he would be willing to take Coleridge into his home to try to cure him of opium addiction: 'I should not have proposed it, but on account of the great importance of the character, as a literary man. His communicative temper will make his society very interesting. . . . ' Gillman, who later wrote a life of Coleridge, proved the right man for the task; it was too late to wean Coleridge off morphine entirely, but he was in caring professional hands. According to one account, written in 1884, he sometimes managed to elude Gillman's watchful eye:

Recently an old labourer here [Highgate], very old and fearing death, sent for the curate of the parish, who discovered that he was using laudanum for his rheumatism, and warned him of the risks he ran. The old man replied: 'Why, I know better, Parson; my brother was doctor's boy to Mr Gillman fifty years or more ago, and there was an old chap there called Colingrigs, or some such name, as Mr Gillman thought he was a-curing of drinking laudanum, and my brother he used to fill a bottle with that stuff from Mr Gillman's own bottles, and hand it to me, and I used to put it under my jacket and give it to h'old Colingrigs, and we did that for years and it never hurted him. . . . ' Mrs Dutton, a charming old lady greatly respected in Highgate, lives in an ivy-covered cottage on the Grove, and remembers Coleridge well. She used to sit on his knee and prattle to him, and she tells how he was followed about the Grove by troops of children for the sake of the sweeties of which his pockets were always full.

Another nineteenth-century writer reported:

The third house in the Grove, facing the church, was a roomy, respectable, brick dwelling, with a good garden behind, and a grand look-out Londonwards. In front of the house is a grove of stately elms, beneath which the poet used to pace in meditative mood, discoursing in unmeaning monologue to some earnest listener like Irving or Hare, or an older friend, like Wordsworth or Lamb. . . . It was in his walks about Highgate that Coleridge one day met Keats. He thus describes him: 'A loose, slack, and not well-dressed youth met me in a lane near Highgate. It was Keats. He was introduced to me, and stayed a minute or so. After he had left us a little way, he ran back and said, "Let me carry away the memory, Mr Coleridge, of having pressed your hand." "There is death in that hand," I said, when Keats was gone; yet this was, I believe, before the consumption showed itself distinctly.'

Lamb frequently visited Coleridge, whom he had known since their schooldays at Christ's Hospital, and referred to him affectionately in an essay on book borrowers:

> To lose a volume to Coleridge carries some sense and meaning in it. You are sure that he will make one hearty meal on your viands, if he can give no account of the platter after it.

Coleridge and Shelley never met, a fact which Coleridge regretted: 'Poor Shelley,' he wrote in 1830, 'it is a pity I think that I never met him. I could have done him good.' Shelley for his part referred to Coleridge in his poem *Letter to Maria Gisborne*, ending with a memorable image of Coleridge's legendary powers of monologue that drove many to the edge of baffled sleep:

> You will see Coleridge – he who sits obscure
> In the exceeding lustre and the pure
> Intense irradiation of a mind,
> Which, with its own internal lightning blind,
> Flags wearily through darkness and despair –
> A cloud-encircled meteor of the air,
> A hooded eagle among blinking owls.

In the last year of his life, Coleridge wrote his own epitaph, carefully re-working it through several drafts in his customary manner:

S. T. Coleridge and the house in Highgate – No. 3 The Grove – where he lived for the last nineteen years of his life. 'My face, unless when animated by immediate eloquence, expresses great sloth – and great, indeed almost idiotic, good nature . . . I cannot breathe thro' my nose – so my mouth, with sensual thick lips, is almost always open.'

Stop, Christian Passer-by! – Stop, child of God,
And read with gentle breast. Beneath this sod
A poet lies, or that which once seem'd he. –
O, lift one thought in prayer for S.T.C.;
That he who many a year with toil of breath
Found death in life, may here find life in death!
Mercy for praise – to be forgiven for fame
He ask'd, and hoped, through Christ. Do thou the same!

He was first buried in Old Highgate Chapel (which became the
chapel of Highgate School), and reburied in St Michael's Church,
South Grove, in 1961. The Gillmans erected a handsome
memorial tablet in St Michael's to 'Samuel Taylor Coleridge,
poet, philosopher, theologian . . . this truly great and good man
. . . the gentlest and kindest teacher; the most engaging home
companion.'

Below St Michael's Church is Highgate Cemetery, the older,
wilder part open only for restricted times because of vandalism.
In the newer part are the graves of George Eliot and Christina
Rossetti. George Eliot's carries the inscription 'Of those immortal
dead who live again / In minds made better by their presence'
from her poem *Oh May I Join the Choir Invisible*, which was quoted
by the preacher at her funeral. Christina Rossetti was buried in
the Rossetti family plot, beside her parents and Dante Gabriel's
wife, Lizzy (see page 165 for the circumstances under which
Lizzy's grave was opened). Her brother, William, was later
also buried there; Dante Gabriel was buried in Birchington,
Kent.

For the final Highgate association we return to the High Street,
where on the outside wall of Waterlow Park, just north of
Lauderdale House, a weather-beaten plaque carries this
inscription:

Four feet below this spot is the stone step formerly the
entrance to the cottage in which lived
    ANDREW MARVELL
    poet, wit and satirist
colleague with John Milton in the Foreign or Latin
Secretaryship during the Commonwealth and for about
twenty years MP for Hull. Born at Winstead, Yorkshire, 31st
March 1621. Died, in London, 18th August 1678, and buried
in the church of St-Giles-in-the-Fields.

Andrew Marvell's house in Highgate High Street as it looked in 1825. (*Mansell Collection*)

Since footsteps might be flagging somewhat by now, and thoughts straying to refreshment rather than poetry, perhaps this is the place for an injection of bracing fervour of the kind to be found in a Victorian guidebook. This quotation is taken from Samuel Carter Hall's *Pilgrimages to English Shrines*, published in 1850 when Marvell's cottage still existed:

> We know nothing more invigorating than to breast the breeze up a hill, with the bright clear sky above, and the crisp ground under foot. The wind of March is as pure champagne to a healthy constitution; and let mountain-men laugh as they will at Highgate Hill, it is no ordinary labour to climb it, and look down upon London from its height. Here, then, are we, opposite the house where lived the satirist, the poet, and the incorruptible patriot . . .

Before wilting, and perhaps seeking a tea shop or 'Ye Olde Gatehouse' pub in North Road (off the High Street parallel to North Grove), it is pleasing to remember that Sir Sydney Waterlow presented Waterlow Park to the public as 'a garden for the gardenless', while Marvell used the English garden as a

115

symbol of the innocence of Eden and also as a refuge for a mind preoccupied with metaphysical anxieties and political problems. In his cottage there was a particular room in which he was said to have worked when he wanted to write 'sense', but when he wrote poetry he did so in the garden. These are two verses from his famous poem *The Garden*:

What wond'rous Life in this I lead!
Ripe Apples drop about my head;
The Luscious Clusters of the Vine
Upon my Mouth do crush their Wine;
The Nectaren, and curious Peach,
Into my hands themselves do reach;
Stumbling with Melons, as I pass,
Insnar'd with Flow'rs, I fall on Grass.

Mean while the Mind, from Pleasures less,
Withdraws into its happiness:
The Mind, that Ocean where each kind
Does streight its own resemblance find;
Yet it creates, transcending these,
Far other Worlds, and other Seas;
Annihilating all that's made
To a green Thought in a green Shade.

CHAPTER 7

Bloomsbury

Not only the Bloomsbury Group, but also associations with Thackeray, Dickens and Shaw, make Bloomsbury seem more immediately connected with prose writers than poets. Many poets have, however, also lived and worked there, inhabiting the elegant eighteenth- and early nineteenth-century houses which have been heavily encroached upon by hotels and the new buildings for London University. But some of its famous squares remain fairly intact, among them Bedford Square, just east of the south end of Tottenham Court Road.

If a disease were to strike the plane trees of London similar to that which has killed so many of the country's elms, it would be a tragedy of the highest order. These handsome, elegant trees grace so many parks and squares, and William Plomer (1903–73) wrote a poem called *The Planes of Bedford Square*. It recalls the summer of 1914 when 'Never were the plane trees loftier, leafier . . .' than

> one afternoon
> warm in the last world-peace before
> the First World War.

Plomer wrote several ballads of London life, including *Mews Flat Mona* about a lady who did 'researches in original sin' on 'a sofa upholstered in panther skin'.

Robert Bridges (1844–1930) lived with his mother at No. 52 Bedford Square from 1877 to 1881, and was visited there by his friend, Gerard Manley Hopkins, when the latter was working as assistant priest at the Farm Street church in Mayfair. During this time Bridges wrote *London Snow* – a magical evocation:

> When men were all asleep the snow came flying,
> In large white flakes falling on the city brown,

Stealthily and perpetually settling and loosely lying,
  Hushing the latest traffic of the drowsy town;
Deadening, muffling, stifling its murmurs failing;
Lazily and incessantly floating down and down:
  Silently sifting and veiling road, roof and railing;
Hiding difference, making unevenness even,
Into angles and crevices softly drifting and sailing.
  All night it fell, and when full inches seven
It lay in the depth of its uncompacted lightness,
The clouds blew off from a high and frosty heaven;
  And all woke earlier for the unaccustomed brightness
Of the winter dawning, the strange unheavenly glare:
The eye marvelled – marvelled at the dazzling whiteness;
  The ear hearkened to the stillness of the solemn air;
No sound of wheel rumbling nor of foot falling,
And the busy morning cries came thin and spare.
  Then boys I heard, as they went to school, calling,
They gathered up the crystal manna to freeze
Their tongues with tasting, their hands with snowballing;
  Or rioted in a drift, plunging up to the knees;
Or peering up from under the white-mossed wonder,
'O look at the trees!' they cried, 'O look at the trees!'

Robert Bridges, who, as a young doctor working in the casualty department of St Bartholomew's Hospital, once saw 30,940 patients in one year.

That is about two-thirds of the poem. In a letter to Bridges, Hopkins (who thought the poem 'a most beautiful and successful piece') claimed that 'O look at the trees!' carried a 'real echo' from his own sonnet, *The Starlight Night*, which Bridges had read. It begins:

Look at the stars! look, look up at the skies!
    O look at all the fire-folk sitting in the air!
    The bright boroughs, the circle-citadels there!
Down in dim woods the diamond delves! the elves'-eyes!
The grey lawns cold where gold, where quickgold lies!

If one turns right out of Bedford Square into Bloomsbury Street, and then left into Great Russell Street, one comes to the British Museum. Laurence Binyon (1869–1943) worked here for forty years in the Department of Prints and Drawings, and lines from his *For the Fallen* are carved on the wall at the entrance as a memorial to the staff of the museum who died in the First World War (see p. 22). Though not specifically a London poem, the opening of his *The Burning of the Leaves* conjures up the autumn ritual of bonfires in the parks:

Now is the time for the burning of the leaves.
They go to the fire; the nostril pricks with smoke . . .

Shelley visited the British Museum on several occasions in the company of Horace Smith, the stockbroker poet who was joint author of *Rejected Addresses*. It was at a time when many Egyptian treasures were being added to the collection, including granite statues of Rameses II and two massive granite columns which bear his name and titles. Smith suggested that they each write a sonnet based on their visits, and Shelley produced the finest he ever wrote – *Ozymandias*:

I met a traveller from an antique land
Who said: Two vast and trunkless legs of stone
Stand in the desert. Near them, on the sand,
Half sunk, a shattered visage lies, whose frown,
And wrinkled lip, and sneer of cold command,
Tell that its sculptor well those passions read
Which yet survive, stamped on these lifeless things,
The hand that mocked them, and the heart that fed:

Memorial carved at the entrance to the British Museum, including lines from Laurence Binyon's *For the Fallen*. (*Longman Picture Library*)

And on the pedestal these words appear:
'My name is Ozymandias, king of kings:
Look on my works, ye Mighty, and despair!'
Nothing beside remains. Round the decay
Of that colossal wreck, boundless and bare
The lone and level sands stretch far away.

Keats was also inspired by the museum's antiquities, and wrote
On Seeing the Elgin Marbles and *Ode on a Grecian Urn*, which ends
with the famous lines:

'Beauty is truth, truth beauty,' – that is all
Ye know on earth, and all ye need to know.

John Keats by the Elgin Marbles (about which he
wrote a sonnet) in the British Museum.

Many stories have been told about the eccentric characters who from time to time work in the Museum's Reading Room, and William Plomer wrote about one 'Seedy old untidy scholar' who each day continued his endeavour 'To fake a universal language / Full of deft abbreviation', in his verses *A Ticket for the Reading Room*; at the end of each afternoon the old man, 'Down at heel and out at elbows', would return to his lodgings for 'Kippers, cake and dark brown tea'. Among the many precious manuscripts and books on display in the galleries are a fifteenth-century *The Canterbury Tales*, the first folio of Shakespeare's plays, and the fifteenth-century manuscript of Malory's *Le Morte Darthur*; and there are also various holograph poems and poets' letters.

No. 38 Great Russell Street used to house Harold Monro's (1879–1932) Poetry Bookshop from some time during the First World War until his death. Himself a poet, he had started the bookshop in 1913 at premises (demolished) off Theobald's Road, and later moved to Great Russell Street. Poetry readings were given there regularly, and the shop became a meeting place for anyone interested in poetry. In 1911 he had founded *Poetry Review*, and he was also responsible for publishing the collections of *Georgian Poetry* edited by Edward Marsh. His own anthology *Twentieth Century Poetry* was an attempt to introduce ordinary readers to modern poetry. He met W. H. Davies at the Bookshop, and the latter came to live at No. 14 Great Russell Street from 1916 to 1922.

Continuing to the end of Great Russell Street, through Bloomsbury Place, one comes to Southampton Row, where John Henry Newman (1801–90), later Cardinal Newman, lived at No. 17 during his childhood. His best-known poem, *The Pillar of Cloud*, which starts 'Lead, Kindly Light' became a popular hymn, while *The Dream of Gerontius* inspired Elgar to write his great oratorio. There is a bronze plaque on the house. Fisher Street leads out of Southampton Row to Red Lion Square where there is a plaque on No. 17 recording that Dante Gabriel Rossetti (1828–82) lived there during 1851, and William Morris (1834–96) and the painter Edward Burne-Jones from 1856 to 1859. Rossetti shared three rooms on the first floor with the painter Walter Deverell, and the landlord stipulated in their lease that lady models must be 'kept under some gentlemanly restraint, as some artists sacrifice the dignity of art to the baseness of passion'. It was here that Lizzy Siddall first sat for him. Rossetti heard that the rooms were again vacant when his friends Morris and Burne-Jones were seeking a London base, and took them round to view. It was the problem of finding furniture for the neglected and dusty premises that turned Morris's mind to designing his own furnishings, and Rossetti reported to the poet William Allingham (1824–89)

> Morris is rather doing the magnificent there and is having some intensely medieval furniture made – tables and chairs like incubi and succubi. He and I have painted the back of a chair with figures and inscriptions in gules and vert and azure, and we are all three going to cover a cabinet with pictures.

Morris and Burne-Jones had a maid known as Red Lion Mary, a tough character who was interested in poetry and painting and willingly used to fix overnight accommodation for all their visitors. Burne-Jones's wife, Georgiana, remembered how 'she cheerfully spread mattresses on the floor for friends who stayed there, and when the mattresses came to an end it was said that she built up beds with boots and portmanteaux'. Rossetti once chanted a stanza from an oriental legend he was reading to Red Lion Mary; it went, 'Shall the hide of a fierce lion be stretched on frame of wood for a daughter's foot to lie on, stained with her father's blood?'. To which Mary replied: 'It shall if you like, sir.' Rossetti remarked to Burne-Jones, 'That's a most remarkable girl, Ned: not one woman in ten would have given an intelligent answer like that to a question.'

Parton Street (demolished) once led off Red Lion Square, and in the late 1930s David Archer ran the Parton Bookshop here which, like the Poetry Bookshop before it, was also a publishing office (the Parton Press) and a place which provided rudimentary accommodation for visiting poets. George Barker (b. 1913), Dylan Thomas (1914–53), and David Gascoyne (b. 1916) were chief among these and after Archer's death Barker published *In Memory of David Archer*, which contains the lines:

> the enormous gold
> urn of your heart
> in which lie the ashes of your friends.

This commemorates Archer's generosity to so many young poets.

Dylan Thomas, with his wife Caitlin, in 1952. Before their marriage in 1937 he wrote to her: 'We'll . . . find a place with a bath and no bugs in Bloomsbury, and be happy there.' (*Press Association Ltd*)

If one exits from Red Lion Square by Princeton Street, turns left at the end into Bedford Row, and then crosses Theobalds Road, one is in Great James Street, where Algernon Charles Swinburne (1837–1909) lived at No. 3 from 1872 to 1875, and again from 1877 to 1878. During this period Swinburne's somewhat irregular life was destroying his health, and it was fortunate that for some of the time the solicitor Theodore Watts-Dunton lived at No. 15, since it was the formation of their steady friendship that in the end saved Swinburne. Their first meeting, however, was not auspicious. Armed with a letter of introduction, Watts-Dunton went to call on the poet; E. F. Benson records:

> He found Swinburne stark naked with his aureole of red hair flying round his head, performing a Dionysiac dance, all by himself in front of a large looking glass. Swinburne perceived the intruder, he rushed at him, and before Mr Watts-Dunton could offer any explanation or deliver his letter of introduction, he was flying in panic helter-skelter down the stairs, and was driven by the enraged Corybant off the premises.

Swinburne's first collection of *Poems and Ballads* caused a great scandal when first published in 1866 – 'he has revealed to the world a mind all aflame with the feverish carnality of a schoolboy' wrote one critic – and was withdrawn by the publishers. He became prey to parodists, and his poem to Our Lady of the Seven Sorrows, *Dolores*, was parodied by A. C. Hilton in *Octopus*, a poem addressed to an octopus at the Crystal Palace Aquarium! Some of his contemporaries, however, saw him as an admired revolutionary, and Edmund Gosse in his biography of Swinburne described him giving celebrated readings in the early 1860s:

> Swinburne in the studio of some painter-friend, quivering with passion as he recited *Itylus* or *Félise* or *Dolores* to a semicircle of worshippers, who were thrilled by the performance to the inmost fibre of their beings. It used to be told that at the close of one such recital the auditors were found to have slipped unconsciously to their knees. The Pre-Raphaelite ladies, in particular, were often excessively moved on these occasions, and once, at least, a crown of laurel, deftly flung by a fair hand, lighted harmoniously upon the effulgent curls of the poet.

Continuing up Great James Street to Millman Street, one comes to Great Ormond Street (on the left) where the Aldeburgh poet George Crabbe (1754–1832) breakfasted with the Lord Chancellor, Edward Thurlow. (There are some attractive Queen Anne houses in the street.) Crabbe's son records that when Crabbe was poor and unknown in London he applied to various great men for assistance, including Lord Thurlow:

To the first letter, which enclosed a copy of verses, Lord Thurlow returned for answer a cold and polite note, regretting that his avocations did not leave him leisure to read verses. The great talents and discriminating judgement of Lord Thurlow made Crabbe feel this repulse with double bitterness; and he addressed to his lordship some strong but not disrespectful lines, intimating that in former times the encouragement of literature had been considered as a duty appertaining to the illustrious station which he held. Of this effusion the lord chancellor took no notice whatsoever.

However a year later he issued the invitation to breakfast, and when Crabbe was leaving handed him a sealed letter containing a banknote for £100. The Hospital for Sick Children, where Robert Bridges was appointed assistant physician in 1878, is in Great Ormond Street. His poem *On a Dead Child* is a reminder of the many tragedies he witnessed during the period he practised as a doctor. He had previously been Casualty Physician of St Bartholomew's and published a report on the shortcomings of a system in which 'it is not unusual for a Casualty Physician to see 150 patients in less than two hours'.

At the west end of Great Ormond Street is Queen Square, where William Morris lived at No. 26 (rebuilt, now the National Hospital) above the workshop of his manufacturing and decorating firm of Morris, Marshall, Faulkner and Co. from 1865 to 1872, after leaving the Red House (see p. 189). During this period, when he was under emotional and philosophical pressures, he frantically wrote *The Life and Death of Jason*, 42,000 lines of rhymed verse – on one occasion producing 700 lines in a day. Henry James went to dinner at Queen Square, and was very struck by Janey Morris:

Imagine a tall lean woman in a long dress of some dead purple stuff, guiltless of hoops (or of anything else, I should say) with a mass of crisp black hair heaped into great wavy projections on each of her temples, a thin pale face, a pair of strange, sad, deep, dark Swinburnean eyes, with great thick black oblique brows, joined in the middle and tucking themselves away under her hair, a mouth like the 'Oriana' in our illustrated Tennyson, a long neck, without any collar, and in lieu thereof some dozen strings of outlandish beads – in fine complete.

After dinner Morris read from *The Earthly Paradise*, and Janey lay on the sofa with a handkerchief over her face, suffering from toothache. When William Cowper was a law student he used to attend the church of St George-the-Martyr in Queen Square, and during that period he was close friends with Edward Thurlow – this being before the latter was elevated to the lord chancellorship. They both used to spend a lot of time at the house of Cowper's uncle and girl cousins in Southampton Row. 'There was I,' Cowper wrote, 'and the future Lord Chancellor, constantly employed from morning to night in giggling and making giggle instead of studying the law.'

Going north out of the east end of Great Ormond Street via Lamb's Conduit Street, one comes to Coram Fields in Guilford Street, with Landsdowne Terrace at the south-west corner. Stephen Spender (b. 1909) was living in Lansdowne Terrace in 1939, and his flat became the publishing office for *Horizon*, edited by Cyril Connolly with Spender assisting. The latter writes:

> To start a literary magazine in September 1939 at first sight seemed an act of mad defiance of historic circumstances. But in fact *Horizon* relieved for its readers the tedium and anxiety of the war. . . . It could make us feel humble that there were pilots in the Battle of Britain who came into our offices to say that they felt they were fighting for whatever *Horizon* represented.

Spender tells how during the bombing the 'flames and the smoke of gigantic fires from the docks' could be 'seen against the silhouetted foreground of Bloomsbury eighteenth-century squares'.

Continuing west, Guilford Street leads to Russell Square, where Thomas Gray (1716–71) had lodgings on the site of what is now the Imperial Hotel when he came to study in the newly-opened British Museum. Edmund Gosse writes:

> his bedroom window looked out on a southwest garden wall, covered with flowering jessamine through June and July. There had been roses, too, in this London garden. Gray must always have flowers about him, and he trudged down to

Covent Garden every day for his sweet peas and pinks and scarlet Martogon lilies, double stocks and flowering marjoram. His drawing-room looked over Bedford Gardens, and a fine stretch of upland fields crowned at last against the sky by the villages of Highgate and Hampstead.

Difficult to picture that now, but the gardens of Russell Square are restfully large and leafy. William Cowper lodged in the square when he was a law student in the early 1750s, and Ralph Waldo Emerson stayed there when he visited England in 1833. No. 24 used to be the offices of the publishing firm Faber and Faber while T. S. Eliot worked there. When Roy Campbell (1902–57) and Dylan Thomas (1914–53) were hard up in the early days of the Second World War and had failed to raise any loans from salaried

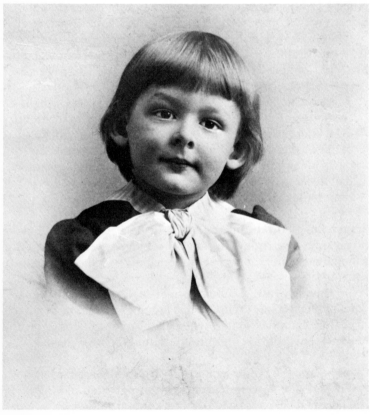

T. S. Eliot at the age of four or five. (*Houghton Library, Harvard University*)

poets working in the nearby Ministry of Information, Campbell
suggested they call on 'His Grace' – meaning Eliot. 'I wouldn't
dare,' said Thomas. But they did, and Campbell reported that
'the great man helped us . . . lavishly'. Stephen Spender has
written that Eliot's conversation resembled the 'Rather drab yet
not unmusical dialogue' that sometimes occurs in his plays; he
particularly recalls the line, 'I daren't take cake, and jam's too
much trouble.' One of Eliot's early poems, *Preludes I*, acutely
evokes a city evening, early in this century; I have always seen it
as London, though it was in fact written while Eliot was a
graduate student at Harvard and before he came to England:

Patrick Heron's portrait of T. S. Eliot, painted in 1949. 'His eyes are lively and
youthful when the cast of his face and the shape of his sentences are formal and
even heavy' (Virginia Woolf). (*National Portrait Gallery*)

The winter evening settles down
With smell of steaks in passageways.
Six o'clock.
The burnt-out ends of smoky days.
And now a gusty shower wraps
The grimy scraps
Of withered leaves about your feet
And newspapers from vacant lots;
The showers beat
On broken blinds and chimney-pots,
And at the corner of the street
A lonely cab-horse steams and stamps.
And then the lighting of the lamps.

When I worked briefly in 1955 for the journal *Time & Tide*, whose offices were in Bloomsbury Street, a lamplighter still came round each evening to turn up the gas lamps; he had bright red hair and rode a bicycle.

A remnant of Torrington Square (just six houses) lies north-west of Russell Square among the buildings of the University (it runs parallel to Malet Street into Byng Place by Gordon Square). Christina Rossetti (1830–94) lived at No. 30 (there is a plaque) from 1877 until her death in 1894. Here her one-time suitor Charles Cayley, whom she had refused to marry on religious grounds, was the only regular gentleman caller, apart from her brother William. Cayley would come to tea and then be invited to stay for a game of whist. In 1870 she had addressed *By Way of Remembrance* to him, but kept it concealed in her desk. It contains the lines:

I love you and you know it – this at least,
  This comfort is mine own in all my pain:
  You know it, and can never doubt again.
And love's mere self is a continual feast:
Not oath of mine nor blessing-word of priest
  Could make my love more certain or more plain.

One of the founders of London University, which dominates this area, was the poet Thomas Campbell (1777–1844), who aimed with other champions of religious liberty to create an undenominational university which would offer 'at a moderate expense the means of education in literature, science, and art'.

No. 9 Gordon Street, which runs off Gordon Square behind University College, was once the home of Charlotte Mew (1869–1928) – the house was destroyed by bombs in 1940. She was one of the poets encouraged by Harold Monro, whose wife Alida here describes Mew's first visit to the Poetry Bookshop:

> On that Tuesday evening in far away November 1915 Charlotte Mew came to the Poetry Bookshop for the first time. Let me try to describe her. The Bookshop itself was a small room about twelve feet square, lined from floor to ceiling with books, and opening on to a dark slummy street off Theobald's Road in Bloomsbury. There would be a number of people wandering about looking at the shelves before going up to the reading room. The reading room itself was a converted workroom that had been originally used by the gold-beaters who occupied a large part of the street: and the gentle thud,thud of their gold-beating hammers rang in the ears of all those who lived there, from morning to night, every day. At about five minutes to six the swing-door of the shop was pushed open and into the room stalked Charlotte Mew. Such a word best describes her walk. She was very small, only about four feet ten inches, very slight, with square shoulders and tiny hands and feet. She always wore a long double-breasted top-coat of tweed with a velvet collar inset. She usually carried a horn-handled umbrella, unrolled, under her arm, as if it were psychologically necessary to her, a weapon against the world. She had very fine white hair that showed traces of once having been a warm brown. Her eyes were a very dark grey, bright with black lashes and highly arched dark eyebrows. Her face was a fine oval, and she always wore a little hard felt pork-pie hat put on very straight.

She lived with her mother and sister in Gordon Street for most of her life, and her poem *The Trees are Down* describes her feelings when the plane trees at the bottom of their garden were felled. These are the last two verses:

> It is not for a moment the Spring is unmade to-day;
> These were great trees it was in them from root to stem:
> When the men with the 'Whoops' and the 'Whoas' have carted
>   the whole of the whispering loveliness away
> Half the Spring, for me, will have gone with them.

It is going now, and my heart has been struck with the hearts
of the planes;
Half my life it has beat with these, in the sun, in the rains,
In the March wind, the May breeze,
In the great gales that came over to them across the roofs from
the great seas.
There was only a quiet rain when they were dying;
They must have heard the sparrows flying,
And the small creeping creatures in the earth where they were
lying –
But I, all day, I heard an angel crying:
'Hurt not the trees'.

Endsleigh Gardens leads off Gordon Street, and runs into
Upper Woburn Place, off which leads Woburn Walk. W. B. Yeats
lived at No. 5 from 1895 to 1919 (when it was known as 18
Woburn Buildings – there is a plaque). In those days it was a
stone-flagged alley and Yeats, who was called 'the toff wot lives
in the Buildings', was said to be the only person there who ever
received letters. Now it is an elegant little pedestrian precinct,
with carefully-restored shop-fronts. Yeats used to be at home to
his friends on Monday evenings from 8 p.m. until the early hours
of Tuesday mornings. Ezra Pound (1885–1972), who met Yeats in
1908 and became a close friend, tended to dominate the
gatherings he attended, laying down the law about poetry and
freely handing round Yeats's cigarettes and Chianti. John
Masefield was another regular visitor, and he called Yeats's
sitting-room 'the most interesting room in London'. The pictures
included several Blake engravings and a Beardsley poster, and
Masefield recalled:

the table bore dark glasses, brown or green, and a dull
red-clay tobacco-jar (with an original dragon embossed on it),
containing cigarettes. The chairs were dark, the effect of the
room was sombre. After 1904–5, he added to the room a big,
dark blue lectern, on which his Kelmscott Chaucer stood,
between enormous candles in big blue wooden sconces.
These candles stood about four feet and were as thick as a
ship's oar. The dim dark blue of this lectern was the most
noticeable colour in the room. He added curtains to match it.

W. B. Yeats, who lived at No. 5 Woburn Walk, Bloomsbury, for twenty-four years. 'He was beautiful to look at with his dark face, its touch of vivid colouring, the night-black hair, the eager dark eyes' (Katherine Tynan).

The Chaucer, produced by William Morris's Kelmscott Press, was one of the last designs on which Morris worked: he drew the borders and initial letters and Edward Burne-Jones did the illustrations. After Yeats married Georgie Hyde-Lees, the sombre objects at Woburn Walk were replaced by the then newly-fashionable unstained wood furniture and earthenware utensils. Ezra Pound was best man at their marriage, which took place at the Register Office, Harrow Road, in 1917. Although twenty years separated the two poets, and Pound nicknamed Yeats 'Uncle William' or 'Old Billyum', their relationship was one of equals. The year after Yeats died, Eliot said in a talk delivered to the Friends of the Irish Academy at the Abbey Theatre:

People have sometimes spoken of him as arrogant and over-bearing. I never found him so: in his conversations with a younger writer I always felt that he offered terms of equality as to a fellow worker, a practitioner of the same mystery. It was, I think, that, unlike many writers, he cared more for poetry than for his own reputation as a poet or his picture of himself as a poet.

Towards the end of his life Yeats remarked to the painter, William Rothenstein: 'When I was young my mind was a grub, my body a butterfly, now in my old age, my body is a grub, my mind a butterfly.'

It was during his early years at Woburn Walk, while still a young man, that *He Wishes for the Cloths of Heaven* was published, with its final, spell-like, couplet:

I have spread my dreams under your feet;
Tread softly because you tread on my dreams.

CHAPTER 8

The West End

> . . . I prefer London to any large town in these islands. . . . In fog
> it is dreadful, but it has many fine days, and in summer . . . its air
> is a balmy air, certainly in the West End. Then it – well the West
> End – is cheerful and quietly handsome, with many fine trees,
> and then there are so many resources, things to go to and hear
> and see and do. Everything is there. No, I think that very much
> may be said for life in London . . .

This is a homesick Gerard Manley Hopkins writing from Dublin
to a friend who had been complaining that he found life in
London to be intolerable. And their exchange typifies the kind of
love/hate relationship many Londoners have with the West End.
There are times when the crowds and the traffic seem to
overwhelm all its attractions; yet when one is away for any length
of time, a desire for Bond Street and all its art galleries, or the
London Library in St James's Square, or the coffee, food and wine
shops along Old Compton Street in Soho, can suddenly seem
overwhelming.

Like everybody else, poets converge on the West End, often
only briefly, and it would be impossible to map more than a
sampling of their visits and residences. The area itself divides
conveniently into five sections – St James's, Mayfair,
Marylebone, North Soho, and Soho proper – of which we will
begin with St James's, where the associations are mainly with
Lord Byron (1788–1824), who is for some people the archetypal
romantic poet of all time. Though, as Disraeli once remarked: 'If
anything was more characteristic of Byron than another, it was
his solid commonsense.'

In the cul-de-sac of St James's Place, which leads west off St
James's Street, Castelmaine House marks the site of No. 22
which for fifty years was the home of the wealthy banker-poet

Samuel Rogers (1763–1855). His house had a fine view over Green Park and he held regular breakfasts to which all the best-known literary figures were invited. It was at a dinner party here that Byron first met Thomas Moore and Thomas Campbell. Rogers himself described the occasion in his *Table Talk*:

> When we sat down to dinner, I asked Byron if he would take soup? 'No; he never took soup.' – 'Would he take some fish?' – 'No; he never took fish.' – Presently I asked if he would eat some mutton? – 'No; he never ate mutton.' – I then asked if he would take a glass of wine? 'No; he never tasted wine.' – It was now necessary to inquire what he *did* eat and drink; and the answer was, 'Nothing but hard biscuits and soda-water.' Unfortunately, neither hard biscuits nor soda-water were at hand; and he dined upon potatoes bruised down on his plate and drenched with vinegar. – My guests stayed till very late, discussing the merits of Walter Scott and Joanna Baillie. – Some days after, meeting Hobhouse, I said to him, 'How long will Lord Byron persevere in his present diet?' He replied, 'Just as long as you continue to notice it.' I did not then know, what I now know to be a fact – that Byron, after leaving my house, had gone to a Club in St James's Street, and eaten a hearty meat-supper.

Rogers was not put off by Byron's affectation (he was a mature forty-eight, and Byron only twenty-three), and after Byron died he wrote affectionately of him in his long poem *Italy*:

> He is now at rest;
> And praise and blame fall on his ear alike,
> Now dull in death. Yes, Byron, thou art gone,
> Gone like a star that thro' the firmament
> Shot and was lost, in its eccentric course
> Dazzling, perplexing. Yet thy heart, methinks,
> Was generous, noble – noble in its scorn
> Of all things low or little; nothing there
> Sordid or servile.

During 1812 Byron lodged at No. 8 St James's Street (rebuilt, now Byron House) near his friend Thomas Hobhouse. It was from here, in February, that he went to make his maiden speech in the House of Lords (see p. 19), and a month later the first

A portrait of Byron, aged 26, wearing Albanian costume; by Thomas Phillips. (*National Portrait Gallery*)

cantos of *Childe Harold's Pilgrimage* were published and he was able to say: 'I awoke one morning and found myself famous.' Lady Caroline Lamb, in common with all fashionable London, read the poem, and she fell in love with the author therewith. A friend told her that Byron had a club foot and bitten fingernails. She was undeterred, and after her first sight of him wrote in her diary: 'Bad, mad and dangerous to know.' Their love affair became an open scandal, terminating with Caroline publicly injuring herself with a knife at a party because Byron had tried to end their relationship. She was, he thought, 'the cleverest, most agreeable, absurd, amiable, perplexing, dangerous, fascinating little being that lives'. When their affair was at its height she used to visit him in St James's Street in the scarlet and sepia livery of her husband's family's page-boys.

Many of the coffee-houses that proliferated in St James's in the eighteenth century gradually turned into private gentlemen's clubs, some of which still exist today. Byron was a member of the Cocoa Tree Club, which was at No. 64 St James's Street, and sent this account to Thomas Moore of a night's drinking there:

> on one occasion, with three other friends of the Cocoa Tree, from six till four, yea, five in the matin. We clareted and champagned till two, then supped, and finished with a kind of Regency punch, composed of Madeira, brandy, and green tea, no real water being admitted therein. There was a night for you! without once quitting the table, excepting to ambulate home, which I did alone, and in utter contempt of a hackney coach . . .

Thackeray wrote this description of club life in the West End as he imagined it had been a century earlier:

> It was too hard, too coarse a life, for the sensitive and sickly Pope. He was the only wit of the day . . . who was not fat; Gay and Thomson were preposterously fat. All that fuddling and punch-drinking, that club and coffee-house boozing, shortened their lives and enlarged the waistcoats of the men of that age.

Byron tended to get fat, too. From 1813 to 1814 he lodged at No. 4 Bennet Street, the first turning west off St James's Street at the Piccadilly end. Here he wrote *The Corsair*, which sold 14,000 copies in a single day, and its sequel, *Lara*, which he said 'I wrote while undressing after coming home from balls and mas-querades, in the year of revelry 1814'. Then in September he became engaged to Annabella Milbanke, a relation of Caroline Lamb's husband. When, two years earlier, Caroline had shown him some of Annabella's verses, he had written: 'She certainly is a very extraordinary girl; who would imagine so much strength and variety of thought under that placid countenance?' Unfortunately these qualities were not sufficient to enable her to cope with the unpredictable Byron. He later cynically catalogued the break-up of their marriage in *Don Juan*:

Don José and the Donna Inez led
  For some time an unhappy sort of life,
Wishing each other, not divorced, but dead;
  They lived respectably as man and wife,
Their conduct was exceedingly well-bred,
  And gave no outward signs of inward strife,
Until at length the smothered fire broke out,
And put the business past all kind of doubt.

For Inez called some druggists and physicians,
  And tried to prove her loving lord was *mad*,
But as he had some lucid intermissions,
  She next decided he was only *bad*;
Yet when they asked her for her depositions,
  No sort of explanation could be had,
Save that her duty both to man and God
Required this conduct – which seemed very odd.

And so it continues for much longer.

Walking northwards up St James's Street one crosses Piccadilly into Albemarle Street, in the Mayfair district, where at No. 50 the publishing house of John Murray have had their premises since Byron's day. Publishing has, like most businesses, changed a great deal in the second half of this century, but just as John Murray dealt closely and personally with Lord Byron, so today his descendant of the same name oversees the publishing of Sir John Betjeman's poems. It was at Albemarle Street that Byron met Sir Walter Scott, and Murray recorded that 'After Scott and he had ended their conversation in the drawing-room, it was a curious sight to see the two greatest poets of the age – both lame – stumping downstairs side by side.' Scott described the meeting in a letter written to Thomas Moore after Byron's death:

It was in the spring of 1815 that, chancing to be in London, I had the advantage of a personal introduction to Lord Byron. Report had prepared me to meet a man of peculiar habits and a quick temper; and I had some doubts whether we were likely to suit each other in society. I was most agreeably disappointed in this respect. I found Lord Byron in the highest degree courteous and even kind. We met for an hour or two almost daily in Mr Murray's drawing-room, and found a great deal to say to each other.

Byron gave the manuscript of his memoirs, entitled *My Life and Adventures*, to Moore, saying that it must not be published while he was alive. The manuscript was lodged with John Murray, and read by various people after Byron's death. Murray and Hobhouse thought it too frank to be published. Representatives of Lady Byron and Augusta Leigh (Byron's half-sister, whom he loved, and by whom he may have had a child) wanted the manuscript suppressed. Moore felt that it should be published, but when a meeting of the interested parties was held he was out-voted, and the manuscript was burned there and then in the fireplace of the drawing-room at 50 Albemarle Street.

Brown's Hotel, in Dover Street which runs parallel to Albemarle Street, was founded by a butler of Lord Byron, and has a room named after Kipling to commemorate his frequent visits there. (Mark Twain also stayed there when on a lecture tour.) Hay Hill leads off Dover Steet, and a right-hand turn brings one to Berkeley Square, where Colley Cibber (1671–1757) lived on the site of No. 19 for the last years of his life. There is a rather unreliable account of the day before he died, but though the detail may be suspect, the spirit is perhaps right:

> A short time before the last hour arrived, Horace Walpole hailed him on his birthday with a good-morrow, and 'I am glad, sir, to see you looking so well.' 'Egad, sir,' replied the old gentleman, all diamonded and powdered and dandified, 'at eighty-four it is well for a man that he can look at all.' . . . And now he crosses Piccadilly and passes through Albemarle Street, slowly but cheerfully, with an eye and a salutation for any pretty woman of his acquaintance, and with a word for any 'good fellow' whose purse he has lightened, or who has lightened his, at dice or whist. And so he turns into the adjacent square; and as his servant closes the door, after admitting him, neither of them wots that the master has passed over the threshold for the last time a living man.

If one exits from Berkeley Square along Bruton Street and proceeds north up New Bond Street, a left-hand turn into Brook Street brings one to South Molton Street on the right (a pleasant pedestrian shopping street). From 1803 to 1821 William and Catherine Blake lived in one room at No. 17. Robert Southey visited Blake here, and the diarist Crabb Robinson recorded on 24 July 1811:

Late to Charles Lamb's. Found a very large party there.
Southey had been with Blake and admired both his designs
and his poetic talents at the same time that he held him for a
decided madman. Blake, he says, spoke of his visions with
the diffidence that is usual with such people and did not
seem to expect that he should be believed. He showed
Southey a perfectly mad poem called *Jerusalem*. Oxford Street
is in Jerusalem.

Robert Southey by an unknown artist. 'The varlet was not an ill-looking knave'
(Byron). (*National Portrait Gallery*)

Unexpectedly, perhaps, Blake during that period was at a party given by Lady Caroline Lamb in 1820, which was recorded in the diary of Lady Charlotte Bury:

> Then there was another eccentric little artist, by name Blake; not a regular professional painter, but one of those persons who follow the art for its own sweet sake, and derive their happiness from its pursuit. He appeared to me to be full of beautiful imaginations and genius; but how far the execution of his designs is equal to the conceptions of his mental vision, I know not, never having seen them. . . . Mr Blake appears unlearned in all that concerns this world, and, from what he said, I should fear he is one of those whose feelings are far superior to his situation in life. He looks care-worn and subdued; but his countenance radiated as he spoke of his favourite pursuit, and he appeared gratified by talking to a person who comprehended his feelings. I can easily imagine that he seldom meets with any one who enters into his views; for they are peculiar, and exalted above the common level of received opinions. . . . Every word he uttered spoke the perfect simplicity of his mind, and his total ignorance of all worldly matters. He told me that Lady Caroline Lamb had been very kind to him. 'Ah!' said he, 'there is a deal of kindness in that lady.'

Just as one might not expect Blake to be invited to a party by Caroline Lamb, so the Northamptonshire poet John Clare (1793–1864) would not be the poet one would expect to witness Byron's funeral procession along Oxford Street:

> While I was in London, the melancholy death of Lord Byron was announced in the public papers, and I saw his remains borne away out of the city on its last journey to that place where fame never comes . . . I happened to see it by chance as I was wandering up Oxford Street . . . when my eye was suddenly arrested by straggling groups of the common people collected together and talking about a funeral. . . . By and by the group collected into about a hundred or more, when the train of a funeral suddenly appeared, on which a young girl that stood by me gave a deep sigh and uttered, 'Poor Lord Byron.' . . . I looked up at the young girl's face. It was dark and beautiful, and I could almost feel in love with

her for the sigh she had uttered for the poet. . . . The
common people felt his merits and his power, and the
common people of a country are the best feelings of a
prophecy of futurity.

This provides an opportunity to juxtapose lyric poems by Byron
and Clare, both of whom, in their different ways, urban and
rural, were at times thought to be mad. Byron was living in exile
in Venice when he wrote a letter to Thomas Moore which
included one of his most famous short poems.

The Carnival – that is, the latter part of it, and sitting up late
o' nights, had knocked me up a little. But it is over – and it is
now Lent, with all its abstinence and sacred music.

The mumming closed with a masked ball at the Fenice,
where I went, as also to most of the ridottos, etc., etc.; and,
though I did not dissipate much upon the whole, yet I find
'the sword wearing out the scabbard', though I have but just
turned the corner of twenty-nine:

So we'll go no more a roving
    So late into the night,
Though the heart be still as loving,
    And the moon be still as bright.

For the sword outwears its sheath,
    And the soul wears out the breast,
And the heart must pause to breathe,
    And Love itself have rest.

Though the night was made for loving,
    And the day returns too soon,
Yet we'll go no more a roving
    By the light of the moon.

Clare, a poor labourer, was forbidden to marry Mary Joyce, the
girl he loved, and wrote poems about his love and loss for many
years afterwards. This is one of them:

No single hour can stand for naught,
No moment-hand can move
But calendars an aching thought
Of my first lonely love.

Where silence doth the loudest call
My secrets to betray,
As moonlight holds the night in thrall,
As suns reveal the day,

I hide it in the silent shades
Till silence finds a tongue,
I make its grave where time invades
Till time becomes a song.

I bid my foolish heart be still,
But hopes will not be chid.
My heart will beat – and burn – and chill,
First love will not be hid.

When summer ceases to be green
And winter bare and blea –
Death may forget what I have been,
But I must cease to be.

When words refuse before the crowd
My Mary's name to give,
The muse in silence sings aloud:
And there my love will live.

Orchard Street runs off the north side of Oxford Street by Selfridge's and leads to Portman Square, where the Poetry Society (see p. 191) used to have its headquarters. The Society took over the publication of *Poetry Review*, and in the late 1940s Muriel Spark (b. 1918), the novelist and poet, was both editor of the *Review* and secretary of the Society. She came into confrontation with the Society's governing council, and left after a stormy Annual General Meeting. Present at the meeting was none other than Marie Stopes, who shook her umbrella violently at Tambimuttu when he made a speech in support of Mrs Spark. J. Meary Tambimuttu edited *Poetry London*, and he approved of Muriel Spark's policy of paying poets properly – a policy which had led to members of the council complaining about the depletion of the Society's funds.

Gloucester Place runs north from Portman Square, and Elizabeth Barrett (1806–61) lived at No. 99 (previously No. 74, there is a plaque) from 1835 to 1838; this was before she met Robert Browning (1812–89). She wrote this description as she watched the sun

Push out through fog with his dilated disk,
And startle the slant roofs and chimney pots
With splashes of fierce colour. Or I saw
Fog only, the great tawny weltering fog,
Involve the passive city, strangle it
Alive, and draw it off into the void,
Spires, bridges, streets and squares, as if a sponge
Had wiped out London.

Dorset Street runs at right-angles to Gloucester Place and No. 13 (rebuilt) was where Elizabeth and Robert Browning had their last home in England during 1855. Elizabeth was writing *Aurora Leigh* at this time, her long romantic verse-novel. From 1865 to 1870 Swinburne lived at No. 22 Dorset Street. During this period friends would send for his father, an elderly admiral, whenever Swinburne's excesses were severely endangering his health, and he would be taken off to the family home in the country to recover. Finally Admiral Swinburne packed up the contents of the Dorset Street rooms and disposed of them, and Swinburne's mother wrote to D. G. Rossetti that their son must not 'take lodgings in town'. But later that year Swinburne moved into rooms in Great James Street (see p. 124).

Working westwards from Dorset Street, through the maze of very attractive streets around Marylebone High Street, one reaches Wimpole Street running between Wigmore Street and Devonshire Street. It was from No. 50 Wimpole Street (rebuilt, there is a plaque) that Elizabeth Barrett eloped with Robert Browning, and where she lived from 1838 to 1846. The play *The Barretts of Wimpole Street*, and its film adaptation, tell the story of the famous elopement. The couple were married secretly at St Marylebone Parish Church on Marylebone Road near the top of the High Street; a window commemorates this event, and there is also a bronze tablet to Browning on the west wall.

Portland Place forms the eastern edge of this Marylebone section, and where it converges with Langham Place is the British Broadcasting Corporation. Over the years the BBC has produced probably thousands of poetry programmes, and among the many poets who worked there were Louis MacNeice (1907–63) and Dylan Thomas (1914–53). MacNeice, who was an imaginative script editor and producer as well as a poet, had a reputation for appearing to be supercilious, and Stephen Spender tells the story in *The Thirties and After* of his attendance

Louis MacNeice at the BBC. He described his work as a radio producer in his long poem *Autumn Sequel*: 'Precalculating microphone and knob / In homage to the human voice.' (*BBC Pictorial Publicity Library*)

at a party given in London during the war by the British Ambassador to Moscow, Archibald Clark Kerr. MacNeice, leaning against the chimneypiece,

> surveyed the party through half-closed eyes, without addressing a word to anyone. As he was leaving the party, Clark Kerr went up to him, and asked: 'Are you Irish?' 'You might call it that,' said MacNeice. 'From the North?' 'Yes.' 'From the East coast?' 'Yes.' 'Well,' said Clark Kerr, 'that confirms the story I have heard that a school of seals went on shore and interbred with the people living on that part of the coast of Ireland.'

Robert Browning and Elizabeth Barrett on the steps of St Marylebone Parish Church, where they were secretly married a week before their elopement.

Thomas's social reputation, as is well known, was for drinking, and while he gave many performances for the BBC in a perfectly sober state, he turned up drunk, once, for a live reading. Roy Campbell was producing the programme, and found Thomas asleep in front of the microphone twenty seconds before the reading was due to begin with Dryden's *Ode on St Cecilia's Day*.

> I shook him awake, and, to his horror and consternation, began announcing him, not in my South African accent, but trying to talk like an English announcer, with my tonsils, in an 'Oxford accent'. Dylan nearly jumped out of his skin with fright and horror, and was almost sober when he got the green light, though he did bungle the title as 'Ode on Shaint Sheshilia Day'; but after that his voice cleared up and I began to breathe again.

In 1946 the actor Richard Burton worked with Thomas in a radio performance of David Jones's (1895–1974) *In Parenthesis*. He remembered the producer saying

> 'Dylan will you take the words Mam! Mam! and scream them for me; you understand that you are dying in No Man's Land, and when you hear the Royal Welch sing, I will give you a cue light and then scream for me would you there's a good chap . . . ' and the green light flickered and Dylan, short, bandy, prime, obese and famous among the bars screamed as I have never heard, but sometimes imagined a scream, and we were all appalled, our pencils silent above the crossword puzzles, and invisible centuries-gone atavistic hair rose on our backs.

Langham Street runs east of the BBC into north Soho, and Ezra Pound had lodgings here in 1908 next to the 'Yorkshire Grey'. During that year, besides producing poetry, he was working on a 'damn bad novel' which he burned. East of Langham Street, off Cleveland Street, is Howland Street, where Arthur Rimbaud (1854–91) and Paul Verlaine (1844–96) lodged at No. 35 during their first stay in London in 1872. (The street, rather a dull one, has been completely rebuilt.) Verlaine finished writing *Romances sans paroles*, and they gave French lessons to support themselves. Charlotte Street runs from Howland Street to Percy Street, where Coventry Patmore (1823–96) lived at No. 14 from 1863 to 1864 when he was working in the printed books department of the

An imaginary portrait of Shelley by David Farris, 1973. 'His features, his whole face, and particularly his head, were in fact, unusually small; yet the last appeared of a remarkable bulk, for his hair was long and bushy, and . . . he often rubbed it fiercely with his hands, or passed his fingers quickly through his locks unconsciously, so that it was singularly wild and rough . . . ' (T. J. Hogg). (*Richard Holmes*)

British Museum. His long poem in praise of married love, *The Angel in the House*, had been published ten years earlier, and his wife had died of consumption, leaving him with six children. He became a Roman Catholic in 1864, and remarried.

Leaving Percy Street by Rathbone Place and continuing west along Oxford Street one reaches Poland Street on the left. Blake lodged at No. 28 from 1785 to 1791, and Shelley and his friend Thomas Hogg stayed at No. 15 after they had been sent down from Oxford in 1811. They were the joint, anonymous, authors of a tract entitled *The Necessity of Atheism*, and Shelley refused to answer questions put to him about it by the university authorities. They had a dark little back sitting-room on the first floor, with trellised vines on the wallpaper. When Hogg left the lodgings, Shelley found it difficult to cope with solitude, and once walked in his sleep as far as Leicester Square. It was during this time that he became friendly with the Westbrook family. Until then, sixteen-year-old Harriet Westbrook had assumed that if she married at all it would be to a clergyman, and she wrote to a friend: 'You may conceive with what horror I first heard that Percy was an atheist.' Shelley, who was nineteen, took it upon himself to liberate Harriet, ending in their ill-fated marriage.

Broadwick Street runs west from Poland Street into Marshall Street, where an inscription on the wall of the steps leading to the modern William Blake House records that this was the site of Blake's birthplace. And finally, at the southern edge of Soho (a district described by the excellent *Blue Guide to London* as 'a centre of gastronomy and dubious entertainment') in the Chinese colony, Gerrard Street runs parallel between Shaftesbury Avenue and Lisle Street, and has a plaque at No. 43 (rebuilt) where Dryden lived from 1686 until his death in 1700. It was here he wrote the *Ode on St Cecilia's Day* which caused problems for Dylan Thomas. It has an opening verse which it is terrifying to contemplate reading aloud in anything other than a sober state:

> From Harmony, from Heav'nly Harmony
>   This Universal Frame began.
>   When Nature underneath a heap
>   Of jarring Atoms lay,
>   And could not heave her Head,
> The tuneful Voice was heard from high,
>   Arise ye more than dead.
> Then cold, and hot, and moist, and dry
>   In order to their stations leap,
>   And Musick's Pow'r obey.
> From Harmony, from Heav'nly Harmony
>   This Universal Frame began:
>   From Harmony to Harmony
> Through all the compass of the Notes it ran,
> The Diapason closing full in Man.

CHAPTER 9

The River

The Thames is all things to all poets. Alan Ross (b. 1922), editor of the excellent *London Magazine* which pays particular attention to poetry, saw 'A zinc afternoon' with 'Phlegm-coloured waves slap slapping / Stone wharves' in his poem *Embankment before Snow*. James Kirkup (b. 1923), in *Chelsea Embankment*, noted that at night 'the lamp's reflections hung / Their ripple-ragged blue and violet anemones, / Snow-berries, amber sea-chrysanthemums . . . ' in the river as it flowed under the bridge. When Kipling wanted to tell the history of London he chose the Thames as his narrator:

> I remember the bat-winged lizard-birds,
> The Age of Ice and the mammoth herds,
> And the giant tigers that stalked them down
> Through Regent's Park into Camden Town.
> And I remember like yesterday
> The earliest Cockney who came my way,
> When he pushed through the forest that lined the Strand,
> With paint on his face and a club in his hand.
> He was death to feather and fin and fur,
> He trapped my beavers at Westminster.
> He netted my salmon, he hunted my deer,
> He killed my herons off Lambeth Pier.
> He fought his neighbour with axes and swords,
> Flint or bronze, at my upper fords,
> While down at Greenwich, for slaves and tin,
> The tall Phoenician ships stole in . . .

And when Michael Drayton wanted to please his patron, Elizabeth I, he set her in a poem about the Thames under the name of Beta:

> And oh! thou silver Thames, O dearest crystal flood!
> Beta alone the phoenix is of all thy watery brood;
> The queen of virgins only she,
> And thou the queen of floods shalt be.
> Range all thy swans, fair Thames, together in a rank,
> And place them duly one by one upon thy stately bank.

This rambling chapter uses the Thames as a link between sites that lie on or near its banks and which do not fall within the scope of earlier chapters. Since it spans a distance of some twenty miles, it would be impossible to visit them all with ease, but the river boats could provide a pleasant mode of transport to a selected few. We start in Deptford (just up river from Greenwich), in Elizabethan times, but in a very different atmosphere from that evoked by Drayton's poem. It isn't the 'silver Thames', but a dark, rural river, running by a small village where Christopher Marlowe (1564–93) went one night and was murdered. The reasons for the killing have never been known for certain, and surmises have varied over the years. In 1598 Francis Meres stated that 'Christopher Marlowe was stabd to death by a bawdy serving-man, a rival of his in his lewde love'. Two years later, William Vaughan reported:

> It so hapned that at Detford, a little village about three miles distant from London, as he [Marlowe] went to stab with his poynard one named Ingram, that had invited him thither to a feast, and was then playing at tables, he [Ingram] quickly perceyving it, so avoyded the thrust, that withal drawing out his dagger for his defence hee stabbed this Marlowe in the eye, in such sort, that his braines comming out at the daggers point, hee shortly after dyed.

At the time of his death Marlowe was under accusation of holding blasphemous opinions, and in 1618 a tract entitled 'The Thunderbolt of God's Wrath Against Hard-hearted and Stiff-necked Sinners' called him 'a filthy play-maker' and exhorted all other 'brain-sicke and prophane poets and players' to note the bad end that befell those 'that live by making fools laugh at sinne and wickednesse'. Nowadays it is thought, through new evidence, that Marlowe may have been a government agent and therefore murdered for political reasons. At all events, he was mourned by his fellow poets and playwrights, and by none more so than Drayton:

> . . . Marlowe, bathed in Thespian springs,
> Had in him those brave translunary things
> That the first poets had; his raptures were
> All air and fire, which made his verses clear;
> For that fine madness still did he retain
> Which rightly should possess a poet's brain.

He was buried in the churchyard of St Nicholas's (rebuilt 1697 and 1957 after bombing), which stands off Creek Road at the juncture of Stowage and Deptford Green. The burial register, which is extant, reads: '1st June, 1593. Christopher Marlowe, slain by Francis Frezer.' There is a modern memorial tablet inside the church. Marlowe was a member of the Earl of Nottingham's theatrical company, which produced most of his plays. These dramatic lines from *The Tragedy of Dr Faustus* are taken from the point when the hour approaches for Faustus to surrender his soul to the Devil:

> Now hast thou but one bare hour to live,
> And then thou must be damned perpetually;
> Stand still you ever-moving spheres of heaven,
> That time may cease, and midnight never come.
> Fair nature's eye, rise, rise again and make
> Perpetual day, or let this hour be but
> A year, a month, a week, a natural day,
> That Faustus may repent and save his soul.
> . . . The stars move still, time runs, the clock will strike,
> The devil will come, and Faustus must be damn'd.
> O I'll leap up to my God: Who pulls me down?
> See see where Christ's blood streams in the firmament.
> One drop would save my soul, half a drop, ah my Christ.

Interestingly, Edith Sitwell referred to this passage in her poem *Still Falls the Rain*, quoted near the beginning of chapter 3. That poem's subtitle is 'The raids, 1940. Night and Dawn', and she includes Marlowe (using the earlier spelling) in this passage:

> Still falls the Rain –
> Then – O Ile leape up to my God: who pulles me doune –
> See, see where Christ's blood streames in the firmament:

It flows from the Brow we nailed upon the tree
Deep to the dying, to the thirsting heart
That holds the fires of the world, – dark-smirched with
  pain . . .

The reference seems particularly apt, bearing in mind that St Nicholas's church was heavily damaged by bombs.

Deptford lies at the bottom of a U-section of the Thames, opposite the area known as the Isle of Dogs, which contains the India and Milwall Docks. At the north-east tip of the U, the Blackwall Tunnel now passes beneath the Thames, carrying dense commuter and commercial traffic and emerging amid stark tower blocks. Once, however, the banks at Blackwall were grassy, and the river yielded rich catches of the silver sprats known as whitebait. Accompanied by more exotic fare, these provided the base for gargantuan open-air feasts, as here described by Shelley's friend, Thomas Love Peacock (1785–1866):

All day we sat, until the sun went down –
'Twas summer, and the Dog-star scorched the town –
At fam'd Blackwall,O Thames! upon thy shore,
Where Lovegrove's tables groan beneath their store;
We feasted full on every famous dish,
Dress'd many ways, of sea and river fish –
Perch, mullet, eels, and salmon, all were there,
And whitebait, daintiest of our fishy fare;
Then meat of many kinds, and venison last,
Quails, fruit and ices, crowned the rich repast.
Thy fields, Champagne, supplied us with our wine,
Madeira's Island, and the rocks of Rhine.
The sun was set, and twilight veiled the land:
Then all stood up, – all who had strength to stand,
And pouring down, of Maraschino, fit
Libations to the gods of wine and wit,
In steam-wing'd chariots, and on iron roads,
Sought the great City and our own abodes.

The success of such a feast would obviously be dependent on fine summer weather, and by way of contrast here is a piece of anonymous doggerel describing one of the frost fairs that used to cover the Thames when, very occasionally, it froze right over. The fair referred to here took place in 1683:

There you may see the coaches swiftly run,
As if beneath the ice were waters none,
And shoals of people everywhere there be,
Just like the herrings in the brackish sea.
And there the quaking watermen will stand ye,
'Kind master, drink your beer, or ale, or brandy;
Walk in, kind sir, this booth it is the chief,
We'll entertain you with a slice of beef.'
Another cries, 'Here, master, they but scoff ye;
Here is a dish of famous new-made coffee.'

A painting by Abraham Houdins of the frozen Thames near London Bridge in 1677. (*London Museum*)

The last frost fair was in the winter of 1813–14, complete with souvenir printing presses on the ice, donkey rides, bookstalls, skittles, dancing booths, sliding barges and merry-go-rounds.

Coming up river into the heart of the city, past Southwark where once the Globe Theatre stood in a hedged field behind the half-timbered, red-tiled houses of Bankside, we come to the parallel railway and road bridges of Blackfriars. The road bridge, built in 1865–69, replaces the one which Dante Gabriel Rossetti overlooked from his balcony flat at No. 14 Chatham Place (demolished) from 1852 to 1862. This site was at the end of what is now the Victoria Embankment, and Rossetti chose the flat so that he could see the sun set over the river and have some privacy to pursue his love life with the copper-haired pre-Raphaelite model, Lizzy Siddall. As well as a romantic setting it was also a smelly one: the covered-in Fleet River, a notorious sewer, emptied into the river near by, and the coal, copper, lime and iron wharves, and most particularly the Gas Light Company's wharf, all had their own peculiar odours. Friends said that on warm days they used to leave Rossetti's parties with sick headaches. Rossetti was more concerned with his work and with Lizzy than with conventionally-salubrious domesticity, though it did not take long for his high-flown romanticism towards Lizzy to fade. When his sister, Christina, made a rare visit to the flat she noticed how Lizzy's face dominated all his paintings, but also how idealized those images were compared to the way Lizzy now actually looked. Christina's observation was expressed in her poem *In an Artist's Studio*:

> One face looks out from all his canvases,
> > One selfsame figure sits or walks or leans:
> > We found her hidden just behind those screens,
> That mirror gave back all her loveliness.
> A queen in opal or in ruby dress,
> > A nameless girl in freshest summer-greens,
> > A saint, an angel – every canvas means
> The same one meaning, neither more nor less.
>
> He feeds upon her face by day and night,
> > And she with true kind eyes looks back on him,
> Fair as the moon and joyful as the light:
> > Not wan with waiting, not with sorrow dim;
> Not as she is, but was when hope shone bright;
> > Not as she is, but as she fills his dream.

Illness, and Rossetti's avoidance of marriage (he had other mistresses), had dimmed the girl whose hair he had once described as 'the golden veil through which he beheld his dreams'; and when he did finally marry her, and their baby was born dead, it was too late to save the relationship. Accustomed to take laudanum, she returned to the flat one night after an early supper with Rossetti and Swinburne, and killed herself with an overdose. Christina had already foreseen the outcome of the relationship in her poem *Wife to Husband*:

> Pardon the faults in me,
>   For the love of years ago:
>   Good-bye.
> I must drift across the sea,
>   I must sink into the snow,
>   I must die.
>
> You can bask in the sun,
>   You can drink wine, and eat:
>   Good-bye.
> I must gird myself and run,
>   Though with unready feet:
>   I must die.
>
> Blank sea to sail upon,
>   Cold bed to sleep in:
>   Good-bye.
> While you clasp, I must be gone
>   For all your weeping:
>   I must die.
>
> A kiss for one friend,
>   And a word for two, –
>   Good-bye: –
> A lock that you must send,
>   A kindness you must do:
>   I must die.
>
> Not a word for you,
>   Not a lock or kiss,
>   Good-bye.
> We, one, must part in two;
>   Verily death is this:
>   I must die.

And Lizzy herself, who wrote sad little ballads, had also been prophetic:

> Laden autumn, here I stand
>   With my sheaves in either hand.
> Speak the word that sets me free,
>   Naught but rest seems good to me.

Rossetti was prostrate with grief and remorse. He could not stay at Chatham Place, returning to his mother's house where, according to Swinburne, 'with sobs and broken speech he protested that he had never really loved or cared for any woman but the wife he had lost'. He secretly placed his manuscript book of poems in her coffin just before the lid was closed, telling a friend afterwards: 'I have often been writing at those poems when Lizzy was ill and suffering, and I might have been attending to her, and now they shall go.' As we shall see later in this chapter, they did not stay buried for ever.

Across Blackfriars Bridge to the south, the second turning west is Stamford Street where Arthur Rimbaud and Paul Verlaine stayed in a room in a boarding house (demolished) in 1874 during their stormy second visit to London. They lived in some squalor and were very poor, taking any available jobs such as one in a cardboard-box factory. Rimbaud had begun *A Season in Hell*, which contains this passage:

> I became adept at simple hallucination: in place of a factory I really saw a mosque, a school of drummers led by angels, carriages on the highways of the sky, a drawing-room at the bottom of a lake; monsters, mysteries . . .

He became impatient with Verlaine's sentimentality and heavy drinking, and they quarrelled and separated. They met again in Brussels, and when Rimbaud tried to leave, Verlaine shot him in the wrist. He was sentenced to two years' hard labour.

About three miles up river, still on the south side, is Battersea Park, laid out in 1852 on the marshy Battersea Fields and altered in 1951 to accommodate the Festival Pleasure Gardens. George Barker (b. 1913) lived for a time across the river in Pimlico, and wrote a poem *Battersea Park* describing a sad walk in November when 'the barges on the Thames / Lie like leviathans in the fog' and the railings and evergreens were pointed with 'Diamonds and pearls like mineral water'. In a more ebullient mood Barker – a prodigious performer of his own poetry – once told an abstemious and over-solemn writer at a pub gathering: 'You need to go on the Big Wheel at Battersea.' Prince of Wales Drive overlooks the south side of the park, and its red-brick mansion flats have housed numerous writers and painters over the years. G. K. Chesterton (1874–1936) lived at 60 Overstrand Mansions for several years at the beginning of this century, and at

Drawing of G. K. Chesterton by James Gunn. 'He grew fatter every year and became more and more a figure of legend, wearing a large flapping hat and an ample cloak, carrying a sword-stick and getting lost on every possible and impossible occasion' (Maisie Ward). (*National Portrait Gallery*)

the general election of 1906 he addressed a huge meeting at Battersea Town Hall on behalf of his Liberal member of parliament. His speech was not a great success; a newspaper reported that he 'prosed on with great deliberation. He as it were, took out his ideas and dandled them as a mother dandles her firstborn', all of which caused the audience to bring his address to a close with shouts of 'Time!'. A coincidence very lightly links

Chesterton with my own family, who lived at Primrose Mansions, Prince of Wales Drive (where I was born) during the early thirties – Chesterton had long since moved to Beaconsfield. My parents had a typewriting and copying office at 25 Victoria Street and one day a large man, somewhat grubby and dishevelled, came in and asked if he could dictate something. My father's secretary was called, and she transposed his words straight on to her typewriter. When he had finished, she handed the paper to him and he walked out of the office with it, muttering under his breath. No one had recognized him, and nothing had been said about payment. Some time later a rather harassed lady rang up asking whether that was the copying office G. K. Chesterton had visited, and if so, could she give the address to which the bill should be sent. His absent-mindedness was notorious; the most famous story being of the time he set out from home to lecture in some midland town, and his wife received a telegram saying: 'Am in Market Harborough. Where ought I to be?'

Beyond Albert and Battersea Bridges, still on the south bank, is St Mary's, the parish church of Battersea (rebuilt 1776), where William and Catherine Blake were married on 18 August 1782, Catherine being the daughter of a Battersea market gardener. The church used to provide Turner with a good vantage point from which to study the effects of sunset on the Thames, and the chair in which he sat at the vestry window has been preserved and restored. During the last years of his life he lived on the other side of Battersea Bridge in Cheyne Walk, Chelsea – one of the most famous streets in London as far as literary and artistic associations are concerned. Although the traffic thundering along the embankment now detracts somewhat from its charm, many of the Georgian houses are carefully preserved, and the back streets between Cheyne Walk and the Kings Road are peaceful and pleasant to walk in.

In the early eighteenth century, when John Gay was secretary to the Duchess of Monmouth who had a house by the river (No. 16 Lawrence Street, off Cheyne Walk, marks the site), Chelsea was still very rural, as demonstrated by Gay's delightful lines about lovers coming out from the city in springtime:

When the sweet-breathing spring unfolds the buds,
Love flies the dusty town for shady woods;
Then . . . Chelsea's meads o'erhear perfidious vows,
And the press'd grass defrauds the grazing cows.

A few years later John Salter, one-time servant of the physician Sir Hans Sloane, opened a coffee-shop on the site of No. 18 Cheyne Walk. Sloane's remarkable collection of objects from all over the world had formed the nucleus of the British Museum, and Salter acquired left-overs from it. His combined museum and coffee-shop became a meeting place for writers such as Addison, Goldsmith, Johnson, Sterne and Sir Richard Steele – who gave Salter the nickname Don Saltero. When Salter wanted to draw attention to his establishment, he wrote a verse-letter to the *Weekly Journal* which began:

> Fifty years since to Chelsea great,
>   From Rodman, on the Irish main,
> I strolled, with maggots in my pate,
>   Where, much improved, they still remain.
>
> Through various employs I've passed –
>   A scraper, virtuoso, projector,
> Tooth-drawer, trimmer, and at last,
>   I'm now a gimcrack whim collector.

His museum collection included, among hundreds of other things, a piece of Solomon's temple, a nun's whip, a pair of garters from South Carolina, a lock of hair of a Goa goat, and Mary Queen of Scots's pincushion.

Lawrence Street leads into Upper Cheyne Row, which was the home of Leigh Hunt (1784–1859) and his large family for seven years from 1833. They were at No. 22, where there is now a plaque. Thomas Carlyle, the Scottish writer and philosopher, was reported by his biographer James Froude to have described the Hunt household thus:

> Nondescript! Unutterable! Mrs Hunt asleep on cushions; four or five beautiful, strange gypsy-looking children running about in undress, whom the lady ordered to get us tea. The eldest boy, Percy, – a sallow, black-haired youth of sixteen, with a kind of dark cotton nightgown on, – went whirling about like a familiar, pervading everything; an indescribable dream-like household. . . . Over the dusty table and ragged carpet lie all kinds of litter, – books, paper, egg-shells, scissors, and, last night when I was there, the torn heart of a half-quarter loaf. His own room above stairs, into which

alone I strive to enter, he keeps cleaner. It has only two
chairs, a bookcase, and a writing-table; yet the noble Hunt
receives you in his Tinkerdom in the spirit of a king,
apologizes for nothing, places you in the best seat, takes a
window-sill himself if there is no other, and then, folding
closer his loose flowing 'muslin cloud' of a printed
nightgown, in which he always writes, commences the
liveliest dialogue on philosophy and the prospect of man . . .

Carlyle was in a position to know the Hunt household well, since
from 1834 to 1881 he lived close by at No. 24 Cheyne Row. (The
house is National Trust property, open to the public at restricted
hours.) A friend visiting Carlyle once noticed two gold
sovereigns on the chimney-piece and asked why they were left
there. Carlyle was reluctant to answer, but finally admitted:
'Well, the fact is, Leigh Hunt likes better to find them there than I
should give them to him.' The friendship between the two
families was immortalized in the poem Hunt wrote after Mrs
Carlyle had impulsively welcomed him with a kiss after he had
been ill for several weeks:

Jenny kissed me when we met,
　　Jumping from the chair she sat in;
Time, you thief, who love to get
　　Sweets into your list, put that in!
Say I'm weary, say I'm sad,
　　Say that health and wealth have missed me,
Say I'm growing old, but add,
　　Jenny kissed me.

Tennyson was among the many writers who used to visit Carlyle
– they would sit up late smoking and talking in the basement at
Cheyne Row – and Carlyle was instrumental in getting a civil list
pension for Tennyson. He approached the politician Richard
Monckton Milnes about the matter, and when Milnes indicated
that it was not something which would find favour with his
constituents, Carlyle replied: 'Richard Milnes, on the Day of
Judgement, when the Lord asks you why you didn't get that
pension for Alfred Tennyson, it will not do to lay blame on your
constituents; it is you that will be damned.'

　　Another story about Carlyle was told by the poet William
Allingham (1824–89), one of the pre-Raphaelite circle. They were

walking together one day and Carlyle said he was considering writing a life of Michelangelo. Allingham responded enthusiastically, at which Carlyle added: 'But, mind ye, I'll no' say much about his *art*.' (In the recording of the two anecdotes, Allingham – an Irishman – obviously found it easier than did Milnes to preserve Carlyle's Scots accent.) It was Allingham who had first spotted Lizzy Siddall working in a milliner's shop and thought she might make a good model for his painter friends. After Lizzy's death, Rossetti never returned to his Blackfriars flat, but decided to lease a house in the street he had long admired – Cheyne Walk. On 23 October 1862 he moved into No. 16 (there is now a plaque), with his brother William, George Meredith (1828–1909), and the young Swinburne as co-tenants. It was, to say the least, a disorderly household. Rossetti had a passion for both old furniture and exotic animals, but not the discipline to care properly for either. Peacocks, armadillos, kangaroos, racoons, wombats, and a zebu were given the run of the place – many of them coming to sticky ends. Swinburne was drinking very heavily, leading to an urge to race around naked, and Rossetti entertained in a careless, lavish manner – sometimes in a large tent in the garden – hoping to attract clients for his paintings. At one point he expressed a desire to keep a young elephant. 'What on earth do you mean to do with him when you have him?' asked Robert Browning. 'I mean him to clean the windows,' said Rossetti, 'and then, when someone passes the house, they will see the elephant cleaning the windows, and will say, "Who lives in that house?" And people will tell them, "Oh, that's a painter called Rossetti." And they will say, "I think I should like to buy one of that man's pictures" – and so they will ring, and come in and buy my pictures.'

Meredith did not survive the menage long, leaving after a supper at which Swinburne declaimed *Leaves of Grass* between courses, and a wombat shared Rossetti's food. Meredith had recently published his sonnet sequence *Modern Love*, a narrative describing how passionate married love can deteriorate into jealousy and unhappiness; it was based on the experience of his own first marriage. These lines are taken from it:

> Thus piteously Love closed what he begat:
> The union of this ever-diverse pair!
> These two were rapid falcons in a snare,
> Condemn'd to do the flitting of a bat.

Lovers beneath the singing sky of May,
They wander'd once; clear as the dew on flowers:
But they fed not on the advancing hours:
Their hearts held cravings for the buried day.
Then each applied to each that fatal knife,
Deep questioning, which probes to endless dole.
Ah, what a dusty answer gets this soul
When hot for certainties in this our life!

Nineteenth-century illustration of Cheyne Walk, Chelsea. D. G. Rossetti lived at
No. 16, sharing his house with a menagerie which included peacocks, wombats
and kangaroos. (*London Library*)

Despite the presence of his earthy mistress Fanny Cornforth, and
his growing obsession for William Morris's wife Janey, Rossetti
was still haunted by Lizzy's death and turned to table-tapping
séances in an attempt to hear her voice from the grave. Some
ambiguous results were achieved. Spiritualism was much in

vogue at the time; the Brownings had experience of it and, while remaining sceptical, Robert wrote about it in *Mr Sludge, 'the Medium'*:

> One does see somewhat when one shuts one's eyes
> If only spots and streaks; tables do tip
> In the oddest way of themselves; and pens, good Lord,
> Who knows if you drive them, or they drive you?

Rossetti began to become more interested in his poetry than his painting, and secretly decided to try to retrieve his manuscript volume from Lizzy's coffin. He arranged for an application to be made to the Home Secretary for the grave in Highgate cemetery to be opened, and finally obtained permission. He was not present at the gruesome ceremony; it is said that Lizzy's long hair was still golden, and the grey calf-bound book intact but saturated. There is a memorial to Rossetti in the shrubbery between Cheyne Walk and the Embankment; the bust showing him with a quill pen and palette was carved by his lifelong friend Ford Madox Brown. A remark made by Morris sums up the ambivalence of his life: 'Sometimes Rossetti was an angel, and sometimes he was a damned scoundrel.'

George Eliot (1819–80) is not usually remembered as a poet, but her verse drama *The Spanish Gypsy* and a volume entitled *The Legend of Jubal, and Other Poems* enable her to be included here. It has to be admitted though that poetry really was not her forte, and even her publisher, who did extremely well from the sale of her novels, while welcoming the manuscript of *Jubal* felt bound to add: 'if you have any lighter pieces written before the sense of what a great author should do for mankind came so strongly upon you, I should like much to look at them'. Her connection with No. 4 Cheyne Walk (there is a plaque) was a sad one. In 1878 her partner, George Henry Lewes, had died, and two years later she agreed to marry their friend and financial adviser, John Cross, who was twenty years her junior. They were married in May 1880, when she was sixty, and on 3 December moved into their new home in Cheyne Walk. On 20 December she developed acute laryngitis, and she died two days later. Cross wrote: 'I am left alone in this new House we meant to be so happy in.'

In 1884 Oscar Wilde (1854–1900) moved into 34 Tite Street, which runs off the Chelsea Embankment, east of Cheyne Walk. He lived there during his marriage until his trial and imprisonment in 1895. His son, Vyvyan Holland, has described Wilde's study and smoking-room:

> To the right of the front door, as one entered the house, was my father's study, in which most of his work was done, at a table that had once belonged to Carlyle. The motif of this room was red and yellow, the walls being painted pale yellow and the woodwork enamelled red; on a red column in one corner stood a cast of the Hermes of Praxiteles. A few small pictures hung upon the walls: a Simeon Solomon, a Monticelli, and Beardsley's exquisite drawing of Mrs Patrick Campbell. But most of the wall-space was occupied by bookshelves, filled with copies of the Greek and Latin classics, French literature and presentation copies of the works of contemporary authors. It was a place of awe, and it was sacrosanct; a place in the vicinity of which no noise was to be made, and which must only be passed on tiptoe.

> My father's smoking-room was, apart from the study, the most awe-inspiring room in the house. It seemed very dark and gloomy to us, but I suppose that it was only dark by contrast to the brightness of the other rooms. The walls were covered with the peculiar wallpaper of that era known as Lincrusta-Walton and had a William Morris pattern of dark red and dull gold; when you poked it with your finger, it popped and split, and your finger might even go through, so this was not much encouraged. The decor was North African. Divans, ottomans, Moorish hangings and lanterns filled the room.

After Wilde's imprisonment for homosexual practices, his two sons never saw him again. They were sent to live abroad under the name Holland, and the contents of the Tite Street house were seized and auctioned to meet debts. Bundles of valuable books were sold for as little as two pounds, and all the boys' toys went for thirty shillings. Vyvyan Holland recalled how in happier times Wilde

> told us all his own written fairy stories suitably adapted for our young minds, and a great many others as well. There was one about the fairies who lived in the great bottles of coloured water that chemists used to put in their windows, with lights

behind them that made them take on all kinds of different shapes. The fairies came down from their bottles at night and played and danced and made pills in the empty shop. Cyril once asked him why he had tears in his eyes when he told us the story of *The Selfish Giant*, and he replied that really beautiful things always made him cry.

In 1900 Hilaire Belloc (1870–1953) came with his wife to live at 104 Cheyne Walk for six years before becoming Liberal MP for South Salford. He worked exceptionally hard, writing on a tremendous variety of subjects which included politics, finance, travel and military science, and could dictate up to 12,000 words during a long morning's work. He was a close friend of G. K. Chesterton, who at that time was living across the river in Battersea. Belloc is probably best known to many people for his children's verses, such as the two that begin: 'The chief defect of Henry King / Was chewing little bits of string', and 'Matilda told such Dreadful Lies, / It made one Gasp and Stretch one's Eyes'.

Long after Swinburne had left Cheyne Walk, and when he was almost dead from too much drink and had gone deaf, Theodore Watts-Dunton took him to live in his villa, The Pines, at No. 11 Putney Hill. This was in 1879 when Swinburne was forty-two, and Watts-Dunton carefully looked after him until he died in 1909. Max Beerbohm visited the household in 1899 and afterwards wrote an essay from which this is taken:

> Swinburne's entry was for me a great moment. Here, suddenly visible in the flesh, was the legendary being. . . . A strange small figure in grey, having an air at once noble and roguish, proud and skittish. My name was roared to him. In shaking his hand, I bowed low, of course – a bow de coeur; and he, in the old aristocratic manner, bowed equally low, but with such swiftness that we narrowly escaped concussion . . .

When they sat down to a meal

> He smiled only to himself and to his plateful of meat, and to the small bottle of Bass's Pale Ale that stood before him – ultimate allowance of one who had erst clashed cymbals in Naxos. This small bottle he eyed often and with enthusiasm, seeming to waver between the rapture of broaching it now and the grandeur of having it to look forward to . . .

Putney Hill is on the south side of the river, an extension of Putney Bridge. Gavin Ewart (b. 1916), who lives in Putney Bridge Road and one of whose volumes of poetry is called *Londoners*, remarked in an essay: ' . . . The Pines still stands on the left side of Putney Hill as you go up it, with a plaque commemorating the poet's residence. From the outside the house looks rather unimpressive. I was disappointed when I first saw it, imagining that it would be bigger and look a good deal more opulent than it does.'

On the other side of the river, just west of Putney Bridge, lies Bishops Park and Fulham Palace. The park, with its plane-lined walk along the river, and the grounds of the palace, are very attractive, and at week-ends there is a lot of sailing and sculling to watch. Between the palace and an adventure playground, and closed to the public – though visible through an iron gate in Bishops Avenue – are the Fulham Palace Meadow allotments, about 400 in all, and the setting for Maureen Duffy's *Taking Down the Runners*, of which this is the first stanza:

Last night the first frost. Time to take down
the twined hop poles of runners, a scene
more favoured of painters than poets.
Backs bend, arms stretch in the labourer's
seasonal gymnastics. Overhead
a jet scores across a pane of frozen sky
on its daily migration. The watering pail's
topped with a glazed lid fallen in the night.
I heft a tendrilled stave. In the middleground
a rout of children riots in shipwreck
through the adventure playground. I shuck off
the stiff green curls, with here and there a hasbeen
that missed the pot like a broken ornament
discarded with the Christmas fir, aware
I am making ritual
out of an annual job.

About one and a half miles up river, past Hammersmith Bridge at No. 26 Upper Mall, is Kelmscott House, the London home of William Morris from 1878 until his death. It is now owned by the William Morris Society as a centre for the study of Morris and his

Gavin Ewart near his home in Putney Bridge Road.

ideas. This extract from the prologue to *The Wanderers* describes medieval London through Morris's idealizing vision:

> Forget six counties overhung with smoke,
> Forget the snorting steam and piston stroke,
> Forget the spreading of the hideous town;
> Think rather of the pack-horse on the down,
> And dream of London, small and white and clean,
> The clear Thames bordered by its gardens green. . . .

He used a similar vision in his Utopian novel *News from Nowhere*, set in the twenty-first century, which opens in Hammersmith with Kelmscott House used as the basis for the Guest House. It was during this period that Morris became involved in socialism, for reasons like this one which he described in a lecture:

> As I sit at work at home, which is at Hammersmith, close to the river, I often hear go past the window some of that ruffianism of which a good deal has been said in the papers of late. . . . As I hear the yells and shrieks and all the degradation cast on the glorious tongue of Shakespeare and Milton, as I see the brutal reckless faces and figures go past me, it rouses recklessness and brutality in me also, and fierce wrath takes possession of me, till I remember, as I hope I mostly do, that it was my good luck only of being born respectable and rich that has put me on this side of the window among delightful books and lovely works of art, and not on the other side, in the empty street, the drink-steeped liquor-shops, the foul and degraded lodgings. What words can say all that means?

Way up river, past Mortlake, Richmond and Kew, Twickenham provides a place well worth visiting to end this chapter, and a complete contrast to the dark Elizabethan association with Deptford which opened it. When Alexander Pope made enough money from his translations of Homer to set himself up in civilized eighteenth-century style, he leased a villa in Twickenham. Unfortunately it was destroyed in the nineteenth century, but it stood in the area where Popes Grove and Grotto

William Morris and his country home, Kelmscott Manor in Oxfordshire, after which his London home, Kelmscott House, Hammersmith, was named.

Road join with Cross Deep. To start with it was a modest affair –
Swift called it a villakin – with 'a central hall with two small
parlours on each side, and corresponding rooms above'. But
during the time Pope lived in it, from 1719 until his death in 1744,
he added 'a brick centre of four floors with wings of three floors,
each story with a single light towards the Thames'. He was also
able to develop the considerable garden, with the help of the
leading landscape architects of the day, in the manner prescribed
in his *Moral Essay* on *The Use of Riches*:

> To build, to plant, whatever you intend,
> To rear the Column, or the Arch to bend,
> To swell the Terras, or to sink the Grot;
> In all, let Nature never be forgot.
> But treat the Goddess like a modest fair,
> Nor over-dress, nor leave her wholly bare;
> Let not each beauty ev'ry where be spy'd,
> Where half the skill is decently to hide.
> He gains all points, who pleasingly confounds,
> Surprizes, varies, and conceals the Bounds.
> Consult the Genius of the Place in all;
> That tells the Waters or to rise, or fall;
> Or helps th'ambitious Hill the heav'ns to scale,
> Or scoops in circling theatres the Vale;
> Calls in the Country, catches op'ning glades,
> Joins willing woods, and varies shades from shades;
> Now breaks or now directs, th'intending Lines;
> Paints as you plant, and, as you work, designs.

He had a perfect opportunity to 'sink the Grot' (create a grotto) in
a passageway leading under the busy Teddington road to an
extension of his gardens on the other side. The embellishments to
this (rare marbles and ores) were later ransacked but it still
survives in the gardens of St Catherine's Convent.

Pope advised on the layout of the gardens of Marble Hill
House, a short walk down river past Eel Pie Island. This is a
Palladian villa, built for a mistress of George II. On the west side
of Marble Hill Park is Montpelier Row, an unspoilt terrace of early
eighteenth-century houses; Walter de la Mare lived in South End
House from 1950 until his death six years later, and Tennyson
lived in Chapel House from 1851 to 1853. His friend, F. T.
Palgrave, was at the time vice-principal of a training college for

teachers in nearby Kneller Hall, Whitton, and the two men used to meet to discuss Palgrave's plans for an anthology of English verse. The plans matured, and *The Golden Treasury of Songs and Lyrics* became famous. Tennyson came to Montpelier Row the year after he was both married and made poet laureate. The latter honour was bestowed 'owing chiefly to Prince Albert's admiration of *In Memoriam*' – the long poem Tennyson wrote over a period of seventeen years following the death of his friend Arthur Hallam. The laureateship meant that he had to write various national and patriotic poems, and the death of the Duke of Wellington quickly brought forth a long ode which was

F. T. Palgrave, compiler of *The Golden Treasury of Songs and Lyrics*. (*Mansell Collection*)

published on the morning of the Duke's funeral, only to meet with 'all but universal deprecation' because of its unconventional form. With hindsight it seems to contain the most conventional Victorian sentiments, though certainly not the even and melodious lines people perhaps expected from Tennyson; they no doubt felt that, as Henry James later expressed it, in this instance 'Tennyson was not Tennysonian.'

In Memoriam contained the flowing rhythms, the merging of sentiment and sorrow with landscape and spirituality that Victorians all over England liked to recite in the drawing-rooms

Alfred Tennyson, photograph by Julia Cameron, *c.* 1867. 'A fine, large-featured, dim-eyed, bronze-coloured, shaggy-headed man is Alfred; dusty, smoky, free and easy, who swims outwardly with great composure in an inarticulate element of tranquil chaos and tobacco smoke' (Thomas Carlyle, quoted by J. A. Froude). (*National Portrait Gallery*)

or read to themselves in their boudoirs and studies. When G. H. Lewes died, George Eliot read the poem over and over again, copying long sections into her diary. Ten years earlier, on New Year's Eve at the stroke of midnight, Lewes had read these stanzas (section 105) out aloud to her:

Ring out, wild bells, to the wild sky,
    The flying cloud, the frosty light:
    The year is dying in the night;
Ring out, wild bells, and let him die.

Ring out the old, ring in the new,
    Ring, happy bells, across the snow:
    The year is going, let him go;
Ring out the false, ring in the true.

Ring out the grief that saps the mind,
    For those that here we see no more;
    Ring out the feud of rich and poor,
Ring in redress to all mankind.

Ring out a slowly dying cause,
    And ancient forms of party strife;
    Ring in the nobler modes of life,
With sweeter manners, purer laws.

Ring out the want, the care, the sin,
    The faithless coldness of the times;
    Ring out, ring out my mournful rhymes,
But ring the fuller minstrel in.

Ring out false pride in place and blood,
    The civic slander and the spite;
    Ring in the love of truth and right,
Ring in the common love of good.

Ring out old shapes of foul disease;
    Ring out the narrowing lust of gold;
    Ring out the thousand wars of old,
Ring in the thousand years of peace.

Ring in the valiant man and free,
    The larger heart, the kindlier hand;
    Ring out the darkness of the land,
Ring in the Christ that is to be.

175

CHAPTER 10

Margents

Originally this chapter was going to be called 'Metroland', referring to the suburbs of west London hymned by Sir John Betjeman, and joined to the centre by the Metropolitan railway line. But most of the sites inconveniently do not fit that category, scattered as they are around several edges of London, and differing widely in character. So, since this is a guide concerned with poetry and the past, 'Margents' was chosen, a word officially described by the Shorter Oxford English Dictionary as poetical and archaic, and meaning 'margins'. The chapter starts at a northern margin of London, Enfield, and follows an anti-clockwise arc, finishing in Bexleyheath to the south-east. It is, however, a very jagged arc, with no linking route; the object being just to make a round-up of some of London's outlying poetical associations. They are all within reasonably easy reach of the centre of London by underground, train or bus.

Enfield Town station has a plaque in the booking-hall commemorating the site of the school Keats attended as a boarder for seven years. In those days it was a country setting, with gardens and cow-pasture, and easy access to the New River. The headmaster's son, Charles Cowden Clarke, taught Keats as much as he could about poetry, music, and painting, and later Keats addressed a thankful *Epistle* to him, from which this is an extract:

> Ah! had I never seen,
> Or known your kindness, what might I have been?
> What my enjoyments in my youthful years,
> Bereft of all that now my life endears?
> And can I e'er these benefits forget?
> And can I e'er repay the friendly debt?
> No, doubly no; – yet should these rhymings please,
> I shall roll on the grass with two-fold ease;

For I have long time been my fancy feeding
With hopes that you would one day think the reading
Of my rough verses not an hour misspent;
Should it e'er be so, what a rich content!

Turning left from the station into the town, Church Street leads to a small road on the right, facing the green, called Gentleman's Row. For two years Charles and Mary Lamb lived in Clarendon Cottage (it was then named The Manse), moving next door in 1829 to a house now called Westwood Cottage. This was so that the haberdasher and his wife who lived there could help look after them, as Mary was oppressed by housekeeping duties. Charles was not very happy in Enfield, being homesick for London and his friends – though many of the latter did walk over for tea, among them Thomas Hood and Leigh Hunt. And the journalist Crabb Robinson recorded in his diary that he once brought with him 'the mighty Walter Savage Landor'. Landor (1775–1864) wrote several epitaphs for himself, including:

I strove with none; for none was worth my strife;
    Nature I loved, and, next to Nature, Art;
I warmed both hands before the fire of life;
    It sinks, and I am ready to depart.

By coincidence, both Keats and Lamb are associated with the next point in this chapter's jagged arc – Edmonton, not far south of Enfield. When Mary Lamb's depressions became progressively worse, Charles came with her to Lamb's Cottage (then Bay Cottage) near the corner of Lion Road and Church Street, just west of Lower Edmonton station, because it was owned by a couple who took in patients. Lamb's *Last Essays of Elia* were published that year, and when friends came to see him he would escort them on their homeward journey as far as the 'Bell Tavern' (demolished) made famous in Cowper's ballad *The Diverting History of John Gilpin*, of which these are the opening verses:

John Gilpin was a citizen
    Of credit and renown,
A train-band captain eke was he
    Of famous London town.

John Gilpin's spouse said to her dear:
  'Though wedded we have been
These twice ten tedious years, yet we
  No holiday have seen.

'To-morrow is our wedding-day,
  And we will then repair
Unto the Bell at Edmonton,
  All in a chaise and pair.'

It was when he was on his way to the 'Bell', eighteen months after moving to Edmonton, that Lamb had the fall which caused his death. He was buried in the churchyard in Church Street, and Mary was buried beside him thirteen years later. Their tombstone is in a paved enclosure on the south-west side of the church. Inside are memorial tablets to Cowper (because of *John Gilpin*) and Lamb – 'the gentle Elia'. Lamb's tablet is inscribed with lines by Wordsworth:

At the centre of his being lodged
A soul by resignation sanctified.
O, he was good, if e'er a good man lived.

Keats Parade, a modern redbrick shopping parade in Church Street, marks the site where Keats lived with his grandmother after his mother's death in 1810. A plaque over a chemist's shop at No. 7 commemorates the cottage where the surgeon lived to whom he was apprenticed for four years. Keats did not like to talk of this period, but during it he managed to complete a fair amount of poetry, while often despairing that he could ever devote enough time to it. As he wrote in *Epistle*, addressed to his brother, George:

Full many a dreary hour have I past,
My brain bewilder'd, and my mind o'ercast
With heaviness; in seasons when I've thought
No spherey strains by me could e'er be caught
From the blue dome . . .

A portrait of Charles Lamb and his sister Mary by F. S. Cary. Cary was head of the Bloomsbury Art School where Dante Gabriel Rossetti was a pupil. (*National Portrait Gallery*)

Stevie Smith (1902–71), whose poem-title *Not Waving but Drowning* has become part of our everyday speech, lived in Palmers Green, not far west of Edmonton. Her address was 1 Avondale Road, which lies between Palmers Green and Southgate and Winchmore Hill stations; a tree-lined road of redbrick houses, with small strips of gardens. Her parents moved there when she was five, and she remained for the rest of her life, attending Palmers Green High School ('The life of the School is based on the essential truth of Christian Principles' says its advertisement in a recent parish magazine), worshipping at St John the Evangelist's near by, and working as a secretary to a publisher. Her life was dramatized in *Stevie*, a play by Hugh Whitemore in which Glenda Jackson successfully interpreted her unique character and manner. Stevie Smith had what has been described as 'a running quarrel with God', questioning the validity of belief and dogma, never more persistently than at the end of *How do you see?*

> Oh Christianity, Christianity,
> That has grown kinder now, as in the political world
> The colonial system grows kinder before it vanishes, are you
>   vanishing?
> Is it not time for you to vanish?
>
> I do not think we shall be able to bear much longer the
>   dishonesty
> Of clinging for comfort to beliefs we do not believe in,
> For comfort, and to be comfortably free of the fear
> Of diminishing good, as if truth were a convenience.
> I think if we do not learn quickly, and learn to teach children,
> To be good without enchantment, without the help
> Of beautiful painted fairy stories pretending to be true,
> Then I think it will be too much for us, the dishonesty,
> And, armed as we are now, we shall kill everybody,
> It will be too much for us, we shall kill everybody.

In 1817 Edgar Allen Poe (1809–49), who had been sent from America by his guardians to have an English education, began a three-year spell at a school on the north side of Stoke Newington Church Street (by Clissold Park, about four miles south of Palmers Green). There is a plaque commemorating him in the

Stoke Newington District Library. In those days it was a leafy, prosperous suburb, with newly-built large houses, as well as older buildings like the mansion which once belonged to Henry VIII 'when his Majesty wished to divert himself with the pleasures of the chase', and the gateway marking the site of the manor house once visited by Queen Elizabeth I, which gave the name Queen Elizabeth's Walk to the old grove of elms by the church. Poe claimed that the historical associations of the place helped to develop his romantic imagination.

Eight miles or so south-west as the crow flies (or, more appropriately from Poe territory, the raven), is the extraordinary expanse of Kensal Green's cemetery, All Souls, girded by gasworks, factories, railway and Wormwood Scrubs. (It is possible, by obtaining a permit from the Canal Office in Delamere Terrace, W2, to approach it along the towpath of the Regent's Canal.) Many of the graves are smothered with saplings, brambles, bracken and grasses – very different from the cemetery's early days in the 1830s when the newly-laid-out fifty-six acres sprouted 'marble obelisks and urns among the cypresses'. Thomas Hood, Leigh Hunt and Thackeray are buried here – the office has numbered maps that give all the graves' locations, though some are still difficult to find in the undergrowth. Hood's son remembered that as the funeral service for his father came to its close, 'a lark rose up, mounting and singing over our heads'. Next to All Souls is the Roman Catholic cemetery of St Mary, where Francis Thompson (1859–1907) is buried. His coffin contained roses from George Meredith's garden with the message, 'A true poet, one of the small band.' The tomb is inscribed with Thompson's line 'Look for me in the nurseries of Heaven'. In his poem *The Kingdom of God*, he suggests that the kingdom is ever present – even in London:

> But (when so sad thou canst not sadder)
> Cry; – and upon thy so sore loss
> Shall shine the traffic of Jacob's ladder
> Pitched betwixt Heaven and Charing Cross.
>
> Yea, in the night, my Soul, my daughter,
> Cry, – clinging Heaven by the hems;
> And lo, Christ walking on the water
> Not of Gennesareth, but Thames!

THE METROPOLITAN UNDERGROUND RAILWAY

PADDINGTON JUNCTION

CHAPEL ST EDGEWARE RD

BAKER STREET

PORTLAND ROAD

SIGNAL MANS STATION
AT KINGS CROSS

The Metropolitan Line, mentioned earlier, now comes into its own, to take us out to Harrow on the Hill. Betjeman's poem *The Metropolitan Railway* is a nostalgic reminder of the days when the 'early electric' was first extended westwards and took young couples away from murky London to the new suburban developments in 'autumn-scented Middlesex'. These are two short quotations from it:

> Smoothly from HARROW, passing PRESTON ROAD,
> They saw the last green fields and misty sky . . .

> . . . They felt so sure on their electric trip
> That Youth and Progress were in partnership.

The first poet specifically associated with Harrow belongs to a pre-electric railway time, and is about as different from Betjeman as one might imagine: Lord Byron. He went to Harrow School (the famous public school that tends to get coupled with Eton) from 1801 to 1805, and spent much time in the nearby churchyard, by the tomb of John Peachey, which he described as 'my favourite spot'. There is a marble plaque near by carrying a verse from his *Lines written beneath an elm*, written at the age of twenty when he was prematurely contemplating being buried there:

> Here might I sleep where all my hopes arose,
> Scene of my youth, and couch of my repose;
> For ever stretch'd beneath this mantling shade,
> Press'd by the turf where once my childhood play'd . . .

Not far from the school, south down the High Street, is Byron Hill where Matthew Arnold lived in Byron House from 1868 to 1873. He moved there from Belgravia with his wife and children because one of his sons, Tommy, who had always been an invalid, was about to go to Harrow School and would need close supervision. Another son had died only a few months before. Arnold tried to look upon the change as a positive one, writing to his mother just before the move:

Sir John Betjeman in front of a poster for the Metropolitan Underground Railway.

I feel more than most people the distracting influence, on
which Byron in one of his letters writes so strongly, of
London society, and am sure I can do most when I am away
from it, though I like it well enough. . . . The kitchen garden
is a well-stocked one, and, I am told, very good and
productive. We gave orders about planting lettuces, as we are
such great salad people . . .

He went on to tell her about the vines, fig trees, and apricots and
peaches, all of which were reputed to ripen two years out of every
three. The grounds of the house have now been broken up for a
housing development, but an old vine survives in one of the new
gardens. The name Byron House must have appealed to Arnold,
for he had admired Byron's poetry deeply when he was young.
He was two when Byron died, so never experienced his influence
directly, but celebrated his debt in these lines:

When Byron's eyes were shut in death,
We bow'd our head and held our breath.
He taught us little: but our soul
Had *felt* him like the thunder's roll.

The family's sojourn in Harrow proved a sad one. Tommy died
after only one term at school, and then some years later
Trevenen, one of Arnold's two surviving sons, became suddenly
ill at the age of eighteen and died within two days. He felt he
could no longer stay in the house, and wrote to his mother:

Everything here reminds me of him so much. He made no
pretensions about liking flowers or anything else, but he was
the one who really cared how the garden was laid out. . . .
Then he never passed a morning without giving an eye all
round the place, seeing how the animals were getting on,
what the gardener was doing, and so on . . .

The jagged arc around London now takes a very lengthy sweep
south-east to 172 Trinity Road, Tooting, where Thomas Hardy
lived from 1878 to 1881; there is a plaque on the house. It was not a
happy time for him: his marriage to his first wife, Emma Lavinia,
was beginning to go wrong, and at one point he was severely ill
from an internal haemorrhage. Evelyn L. Evans describes the
period:

Matthew Arnold. 'He was tall, of commanding presence, with black hair, which never became grey, and blue eyes. He was short-sighted, and his eye-glass gave him a false air of superciliousness. In reality he was the most genial and amiable of men' (Herbert Paul). (*Trustees of Dove Cottage, Grasmere*)

Certainly he advanced socially, being elected to both the Savile and the Rabelais Clubs, and meeting such leading figures as Tennyson, Browning, Arnold and Henry James. But he would lie awake in his Upper Tooting house, feeling the 'close proximity to a monster whose body had four million heads and eight million eyes'.

A scene near Tooting Common prompted his poem *Beyond the Last Lamp*, of which these are the first two verses:

While rain, with eve in partnership,
Descended darkly, drip, drip, drip,
Beyond the last lone lamp I passed
    Walking slowly, whispering sadly,
    Two linked loiterers, wan, downcast:
Some heavy thought constrained each face,
And blinded them to time and place.

The pair seemed lovers, yet absorbed
In mental scenes no longer orbed
By love's young rays. Each countenance
    As it slowly, as it sadly
    Caught the lamplight's yellow glance,
Held in suspense a misery
At things which had been or might be.

Like Thomas Hardy, D. H. Lawrence is better known for his novels, but in his poetry he left sharp, evocative descriptions of his personal life. When he was twenty-three he came south to teach in a new school, Davidson High School, in Croydon, several miles south-east of Tooting. During the time he was there, 1908 to 1912, Croydon was a fast-expanding suburb, recorded in Lawrence's *Flat Suburbs, S.W., in the Morning*:

The new red houses spring like plants
    In level rows
Of reddish herbage that bristles and slants
    Its square shadows.

The pink young houses show one side bright
    Flatly assuming the sun,
And one side shadow, half in sight,
    Half-hiding the pavement-run;

Where hastening creatures pass intent
    On their level way,
Threading like ants that can never relent
    And have nothing to say.

Bare stems of street lamps stiffly stand
   At random, desolate twigs,
To testify to a blight on the land
   That has stripped their sprigs.

His first lodgings were at 12 Colworth Road, off Addiscombe
Road, and he reported that 'my landlady is a splendid woman –
my landlord is affable and plays chess worse than I do – what
more can I want?' One day, when he was sitting in the
dining-room, he wrote to a friend:

> You know we are on the very edge of the town; there are
> great trees on the Addiscombe Road, at the end of Colworth.
> Here, in this room, there is a glass door, opening onto our
> little garden. Beyond the grey board fence at the bottom rises
> the embankment, a quiet, grassy embankment of a light
> railway that runs from the great lines – S.E. and the London,
> Brighton. In the dark, as if suspended in the air, little trains
> pass bright and yellow across the uncurtained door.

In the autumn of 1911 he moved with friends into No. 16
Colworth Road, where things were not so comfortable:

> You know we're living here in the kitchen, small and bare
> and ugly, because the electric isn't connected up – all too poor
> to have it done – truth.

He became very ill, and the following year had to resign his post.
He had been a sympathetic teacher, as can be deduced from the
poems he wrote about Davidson School. Some of his pupils came
from an orphanage, and on a snowy day he noticed them

> Clinging to the radiators, like numbed bees to the drenched
>   grass,
> The boys from the Home, blue and inanimate . . .

And in *The Best of School* he described the pleasure of that rare
occasion when a whole class is happily absorbed in their work:

> The blinds are drawn because of the sun,
> And the boys and the room in a colourless gloom
> Of underwater float: bright ripples run

Across the walls as the blinds are blown
To let the sunlight in; and I,
As I sit on the shores of the class, alone,
Watch the boys in their summer blouses
As they write, their round heads busily bowed:
And one after another rouses
His face to look at me,
To ponder very quietly,
As seeing, he does not see.

And then he turns again, with a little, glad
Thrill of his work he turns again from me,
Having found what he wanted, having got what was to be
    had.

And very sweet it is, while the sunlight waves
In the ripening morning, to sit alone with the class
And feel the stream of awakening ripple and pass
From me to the boys, whose brightening souls it laves
For this little hour.

The word 'anerly' is an old-fashioned, dialect term for 'only' or 'only just' – a vague, melodic word. The suburb Anerley, north of Croydon between the harsher-named Penge and Norwood, was the home for the first twenty-five years of this century of Walter de la Mare (1873–1956), and somehow this flowing, insubstantial word exactly suits the nature of his poetry. It is impossible to link anecdote and place to specific verses which he wrote, for they nearly all seem to happen in a dream world, which made him particularly successful with children because, as he said, 'between their dream and their reality looms no impassable abyss'. *A Young Girl* described the abyss that occurs once adulthood is reached:

I search in vain your childlike face to see
The thoughts that hide behind the words you say;
I hear them singing, but close-shut from me
Dream the enchanted woods through which they stray.
Cheek, lip, and brow – I glance from each to each,
And watch that light-winged Mercury, your hand;
And sometimes when brief silence falls on speech
I seem your hidden self to understand.

Mine a dark fate. Behind his iron bars
The captive broods, with ear and heart astrain

For jangle of key, for glimpse of moon or stars,
Grey shaft of daybreak, sighing of the rain.
Life built these walls. Past all my dull surmise
Must burn the inward innocence of your eyes.

During the period de la Mare lived in Anerley he had three addresses, the last of which (1912–25) was 14 Thornsett Road.

In Bexleyheath, north-east of Anerley, is the house which William Morris built in 1859 when he married Jane Burden, the dark-haired beauty who modelled for the pre-Raphaelites. Called Red House because of its brick fabric and red roofs, it embodies Morris's principles of domestic architecture (Philip Webb was the architect) and has decorations and furnishings by members of the pre-Raphaelite group. It is in Red House Lane, off Upton Road, and is open to the public the first Saturday and Sunday of the month, from 2.30–4.30. When it was first built it had wide views over the Cray valley, and was set in an orchard so near the trees that on hot autumn nights apples fell in through the open windows. There were long grass walks, with lilies and sunflowers, and for five years it was a place where the ideals and loves of the Morrises and their friends flourished and faded. In the end Morris had to return to central London in order to pursue his work effectively, a move which coincided with Janey's decreasing affection. Jack Lindsay, Morris's biographer, writes:

Morris could never bear to go and look at Red House again. He was in fact leaving much more behind than he could have known at the time. With the loss of the dream of recreating around himself a medieval world he also lost the love of the woman who had been for him the incarnation of that dream.

Morris was able to design and erect his own dream, but to less well-endowed mortals the vision of suburbia has been presented and sold as a packaged commodity. Nor is this a twentieth-century phenomenon, as these lines from George Colman's (1762–1836) *Suburbia* demonstrate:

Where the prig architect, with *style* in view,
Has doled his houses forth, in two by two;
And rear'd a row upon the plan, no doubt,
Of old men's jaws, with every third tooth out.
Or where, still greater lengths in taste to go,

He warps his tenements into a bow;
Nails a scant canvas, propt in slight deal sticks,
Nick-named *veranda*, to the first-floor bricks;
Before the whole, in one smug segment drawn,
Claps half a rood of turf he calls a lawn;
Then, chuckling at his lath-and-plaster bubble,
Dubs it the CRESCENT, – and the rents are double.

Over a century later, Betjeman looked on the habits and
pretensions of suburbia with a more kindly eye, and never more
so than in *Middlesex* where he describes a young office worker
going home to Ruislip, an area he had known in its more rural
days when he walked by the river Brent.

Gaily into Ruislip Gardens
   Runs the red electric train,
With a thousand Ta's and Pardon's
   Daintily alights Elaine;
Hurries down the concrete station
With a frown of concentration,
Out into the outskirt's edges
Where a few surviving hedges
Keep alive our lost Elysium – rural Middlesex again.

Well cut Windsmoor flapping lightly,
   Jacqmar scarf of mauve and green
Hiding hair which, Friday nightly,
   Delicately drowns in Drene;
Fair Elaine the bobby-soxer,
Fresh-complexioned with Innoxa,
Gains the garden – father's hobby –
Hangs her Windsmoor in the lobby,
Settles down to sandwich supper and the television screen.

Gentle Brent, I used to know you
   Wandering Wembley-wards at will,
Now what change your waters show you
   In the meadowlands you fill!
Recollect the elm-trees misty
And the footpath climbing twisty
Under cedar-shaded palings,
Low laburnum-leaned-on railings,
Out of Northolt on and upwards to the heights of Harrow hill.

CHAPTER 11

Poetry now

Poetry readings and workshops take place in dozens of bookshops, bars, colleges and community centres all over London. Since the groups who organize such activities tend to come and go, a list of centres that are active as this guide is written would be of limited use in a year's time. But there are easy ways for the visitor to find out what is happening.

The weekly publication *Time Out* (trusting that it will flourish for a long time to come) is invaluable for practically every kind of entertainment, and a lot more beside; it includes a section on poetry readings, workshops, publications and (occasionally) bookshops. Virtually all the readings and many of the workshops are' open to the general public.

The Arts Council of Great Britain has a library of modern poetry at 9 Long Acre, Covent Garden, WC2, telephone 01-379 6597, which is open Tuesday–Saturday 10a.m.–5p.m., and Friday until 7p.m. Anyone may call in and look around, or join and borrow up to four books at a time, free of charge. The library also has literary periodicals, pamphlets and information about activities currently taking place. It is next door to the Arts Council Shop which sells books, art catalogues, posters, museum postcards, etc. and displays information about arts activities.

Each region of Britain has its own arts association, the one for London being the Greater London Arts Association at 25/31 Tavistock Place, WC1, telephone 01-388 2211. It is the headquarters of the London Poetry Secretariat, which arranges poetry readings all over London, and will have information on activities currently taking place.

The National Poetry Centre at 21 Earls Court Square (near Earls Court underground), SW5, telephone 01-373 7861, holds a variety of readings, events and workshops. It is the headquarters of the Poetry Society which publishes the *Poetry Review*. The

Poets' London

A poetry reading at the National Poetry Centre, 21 Earls Court Square.

Centre has a printshop where members of the public (by arrangement) may reproduce their work, and a bookshop which carries a wide range of poetry from small and independent presses. There is a bar which is open when readings take place.

The National Book League, 7 Albemarle Street, W1, off Piccadilly, telephone 01-493 9001, exists to promote books and reading generally. It organizes many exhibitions and will answer queries from the general public. Various services and facilities (including a restaurant and bar) are available to its members.

As well as the local and informal poetry workshops which take place all over London, there are flourishing (and inexpensive) writing classes – including poetry – available at Morley College, 61 Westminster Bridge Road, SE1, telephone 01-928 8501, and The City Literary Institute (known as The City Lit), Stukeley Street, Drury Lane, WC2, telephone 01-242 9872. These courses are run by practising professional writers.

While it is comparatively easy to find the works of very well-known poets in bookshops, the distribution of publications by less-established poets is very patchy. This is partly due to the fact that nearly all such publications emanate from small publishers who do not have a wide distribution network, and also because booksellers are not always willing to devote space to pamphlets and slim volumes. Some bookshops make a point of stocking such publications: the one at the National Poetry Centre has already been mentioned, and two others are Compendium, 240 Camden High Street, NW1, and Centerprise, 136 Kingsland High Street, E8. Centerprise is a noteworthy organization for anyone interested in community publishing as it prints and sells writing by people living locally in London's east end. The literature officer at the Greater London Arts Association will have details of similar community bookshops and publishing ventures in other parts of London. For paperback volumes of established writers from major publishers, the basement of Hatchards bookshop, 187 Piccadilly, W1, may be recommended for efficiency and knowledgeable staff. And visitors to the large department stores may like to know that Harrods has an extensive book department, and Selfridges a smaller but quite imaginative one; both stock poetry. There are of course hundreds

Part of the literature section of the London Library, St James's Square. The library contains approximately one million books.

of bookshops in Greater London, and people who stay for any length of time will discover their own favourites.

Such people will also probably make use of the excellent free public library system, and scholars in search of rare books will find their way to the Reading Room of the British Museum. Rather less well known, and admittedly only available for a substantial annual subscription (£36 in 1979), is the London Library at 14 St James's Square, SW1, telephone 01-930 7705. This is an institution to which hundreds of writers, scholars and readers pledge utter devotion. It was founded by Thomas Carlyle and colleagues in 1841 in order that its members might have direct access to the shelves of a fine library and be able to take books home with them. This means that a member may wander through a collection of nearly a million books, take his or her ease in the comfortable reading room, and carry away up to ten volumes. The staff are helpful, and the literature section contains thousands of volumes of poetry, many of them in old editions.

Perhaps to end this short section, a personal view of poetry readings in general would not be out of place. They are not always comfortable events. You can't, as a member of the audience, feel quite as anonymous as you can in a cinema or a concert hall. You may be exhilarated, embarrassed, bored, or even angered by the words emanating from the poet addressing you; he or she may pronounce those words movingly, expressionlessly, or eloquently; there may be three or 300 people present; the room may be dingy or elegant; and all the factors that influence one's own mood may make it difficult to concentrate. However, weighted against those occasions when the ingredients don't quite flow together to forge a unique and exciting experience, are the ones when the language and voice combine to make a perfect vehicle for the ideas and emotions the poet is striving to express, and the result is embedded in the hearer's mind for ever. It is always worth going to hear poets one admires read their own work, and often illuminating to hear intelligent readers interpret other people's poems. Dylan Thomas was probably the most famous reader of his own work in this century, and in these lines from *Autumn Sequel*, written after Thomas's death, Louis MacNeice describes the effect of his voice and presence. Gwilym is the name which he gave to Dylan in the poem.

And did we once see Gwilym plain? We did.

And heard him even plainer. A whole masque
Of tones and cadences – the organ boom,
The mimicry, then the chuckles; we could bask

As though in a lush meadow in any room
Where that voice started, trellising the air
With honeysuckle or dog-rose, bloom on bloom,

And loosing bees between them and a bear
To grumble after the bees. Such rooms are still
Open to us but now are merely spare

Rooms and in several senses: damp and chill
With dust-sheets over the furniture and the voice
Silent, the meadow vanished, the magic nil.

Those baffled by the sheer number of poets who may be
sampled in print and in person, might like to take comfort from
Anthony Thwaite's (b. 1930) comic poem *On consulting
'Contemporary Poets of the English Language'*, extracts from which
bring this guide to an end. Ideally the poem needs to be chanted
out aloud (Thwaite performs it at top speed) – perhaps with
friends over a drink after a long ramble around poets' London. It
takes a bit of practice to become fluent because of the rhythm
changes – rather like dancing to a disc which keeps changing
time. Allow the beat and the rhyme to dictate the pronunciation.

Dannie Abse, Douglas Dunn,
Andrew Waterman, Thom Gunn,
Peter Redgrove, Gavin Ewart,
Susan Fromberg Schaeffer, Stewart
Conn, Pete Brown, Elizabeth
Jennings, Jim Burns, George MacBeth
. . .
Norman Hidden, David Wright,
Philip Larkin, Ivan White,
Stephen Spender, Tom McGrath,
dom sylvester houédard,
A. Alvarez, Herbert Lomas,
D.M., R.S., Donald Thomas,
Causley, Cunningham, Wes Magee,
Silkin, Simmons, Laurie Lee

. . .

Fullers both and Joneses all,
Donald Davie, Donald Hall,
Muldoon, Middleton, Murphy, Miller,
Tomlinson, Tonks, Turnbull, Tiller,
Barker, Brownjohn, Blackburn, Bell,
Kirkup, Kavanagh, Kendrick, Kell,
McGough, MacLean, MacSweeney, Schmidt,
Hughes (of *Crow*) and (of *Millstone Grit*)

. . .

Betjeman, Nicholson, Grigson, Walker,
Pitter, Amis, Hilary Corke, a
Decad of Smiths, a Potts and a Black,
Roberts Conquest, Mezey, Graves and Pack,
Hugh MacDiarmid (C.M. Grieve's
His real name, of course), James Reeves,
Durrell, Gershon, Harwood, Mahon,
Edmond Wright, Nathaniel Tarn,
Sergeant, Snodgrass, C.K. Stead,
William Shakespeare (no, he's dead),
Cole and Mole and Lowell and Bly,
Robert Nye and Atukwei Okai,
Christopher Fry and George Mackay
Brown, Wayne Brown, John Wain, K. Raine,
Jenny Joseph, Jeni Couzyn,
D.J. Enright, J.C. Hall,
C.H. Sisson and all and all . . .
What is it, you may ask, that Thwaite's
Up to in this epic? Yeats'
Remark in the Cheshire Cheese one night
With poets so thick they blocked the light:
'No one can tell who has talent, if any.
Only one thing is certain. We are too many.'

Appendix: List of authors mentioned in text

A list of authors mentioned in this guide, together with selected titles of their works. The titles include single poems, collections of poetry, and plays partly or wholly in verse. Prose titles are not included, although a few of the authors are equally or better known as prose writers.

Addison, Joseph (1672–1719). Poet, playwright, essayist. *The Campaign*.

Akenside, Mark (1721–70). Physician, poet. *The Pleasures of Imagination*.

Allingham, William (1824–89). Poet, customs official. *Spring; Meadowsweet*.

Arnold, Matthew (1822–88). Poet, critic, inspector of schools. *The Forsaken Merman; Sohrab and Rustum; Dover Beach; The Scholar Gipsy*.

Auden, Wystan Hugh (1907–73). Poet, librettist. *Lay your sleeping head, my love; The Shield of Achilles; About the House*.

Baillie, Joanna (1762–1851). Poet, playwright. *Fugitive Verses; Metrical Legends*.

Barker, George (b. 1913). Poet. *The True Confession of George Barker; Calamiterror*.

Behn, Aphra (1640–89). Playwright, novelist, poet. *The Rover; Pindarick Poem on the Happy Coronation*.

Belloc, Hilaire (1870–1953). Essayist, novelist, biographer, critic, poet, politician. *The Bad Child's Book of Beasts; Cautionary Tales*.

Betjeman, Sir John (b. 1906). Poet, building preservationist. *A Few Late Chrysanthemums; Summoned by Bells; A Subaltern's Love-song*.

Binyon, Laurence (1869–1943). Poet, art historian. *For the Fallen; The Burning of the Leaves*.

Blake, William (1757–1827). Poet, painter, engraver. *Songs of Innocence; Songs of Experience; Jerusalem.*

Bloomfield, Robert (1766–1823). Poet, shoemaker. *The Farmer's Boy.*

Bridges, Robert (1844–1930). Poet, doctor. *The Growth of Love; London Snow; The Testament of Beauty.*

Brontë, Anne (1820–49). Novelist, poet. *If This Be All.*

Brontë, Charlotte (1816–55). Novelist, poet. *Parting; The Letter.*

Brontë, Emily (1818–48). Novelist, poet. *Sleep not, dream not; The night is darkening; Remembrance.*

Browning, Elizabeth Barrett (1806–61). Poet. *Sonnets from the Portuguese; Aurora Leigh.*

Browning, Robert (1812–89). Poet, playwright. *My Last Duchess; Andrea del Sarto; The Ring and the Book; Home-thoughts from Abroad.*

Burns, Robert (1759–96). Poet, farmer. *To a Mouse; To a Mountain Daisy; Tam o'Shanter; A Red, Red Rose.*

Butler, Samuel (1612–80). Poet, secretary, satirist. *Hudibras.*

Byron, George Gordon, 6th Baron (1788–1824). Poet. *Childe Harold's Pilgrimage; Don Juan; The Vision of Judgment; So, We'll Go No More a Roving; Destruction of Sennacherib.*

Caedmon (active 670). Herdsman, poet. *Hymn.*

Campbell, Roy (1902–57). Poet, jack-of-all-trades. *The Flaming Terrapin; Adamastor; The Zebras.*

Campbell, Thomas (1777–1844). Poet, reformer. *The Pleasures of Hope; Hohenlinden; Ye Mariners of England.*

Campion, Thomas (d. 1620). Poet, physician, musician. *Four Books of Ayres.*

Carew, Thomas (*c.* 1598–*c.* 1639). Courtier, poet. *Coelum Britannicum; The Rapture.*

Chapman, George (*c.* 1559–1634). Poet, translator, playwright. *The Shadow of Night,* translations of Homer.

Chatterton, Thomas (1752–70). Poet. *Poems supposed to have been written at Bristol, by Thomas Rowley and others, in the Fifteenth Century; The Revenge: a Burletta.*

Chaucer, Geoffrey (*c.* 1343–1400). Poet, court official. *The Canterbury Tales; Troylus and Cryseyde; The Legende of Good Women.*

Chesterton, Gilbert Keith (1874–1936). Essayist, critic, novelist, poet. *Lepanto; The Donkey.*

Church, Richard (1893–1972). Poet, novelist. *The Inheritors; The Burning Bush.*

Churchill, Charles (1731–64). Poet, clergyman. *The Rosciad; The Prophecy of Famine.*

Cibber, Colley (1671–1757). Actor, playwright, poet. *The Blind Boy; Damon and Phillida.*

Clare, John (1793–1864). Poet, farmer. *Poems Descriptive of Rural Life; The Village Minstrel; The Shepherd's Calendar.*

Coleridge, Samuel Taylor (1772–1834). Poet, philosopher, critic, playwright. *The Ancient Mariner; Kubla Khan; Christabel.*

Colman, George, the Younger (1762–1836). Playwright, poet. *Poetical Vagaries; Vagaries vindicated, or Hypocritic Hypercritics.*

Cowley, Abraham (1618–67). Poet, essayist, diplomat. *The Mistress; The Miscellanies.*

Cowper, William (1731–1800). Poet. *The Task; John Gilpin; On the Receipt of My Mother's Picture.*

Crabbe, George (1754–1832). Poet, parson. *The Village; The Parish Register; Sir Eustace Grey.*

D'Avenant, Sir William (1606–68). Playwright, poet. *Gondibert.*

Davidson, John (1857–1909). Poet, playwright. *Fleet Street Eclogues; Ballads and Songs.*

Davies, William Henry (1871–1940). Poet, autobiographer. *An Old House in London; Leisure.*

Day Lewis, Cecil (1904–72). Poet, translator, detective story writer. *An Italian Journey; You That Love England.*

Dekker, Thomas (*c.* 1570–1632). Playwright, pamphleteer. *Patient Grissil; The Shoemaker's Holiday.*

De la Mare, Walter (1873–1956). Poet, novelist. *The Fleeting; The Listeners; Peacock Pie.*

Donne, John (*c.* 1572–1631). Poet, preacher. *The Ecstasy; Death be not Proud; Go, and catch a falling star; To his Mistress Going to Bed; A Valediction: forbidding Mourning; Lovers' Infiniteness.*

Dowson, Ernest (1867–1900). Poet. *I have been faithful to thee, Cynara! in my fashion; They are not long, the weeping and the laughter.*

Drayton, Michael (1563–1631). Poet. *Polyolbion; Ballad of Agincourt; Since there's no help, come let us kiss and part.*

Dryden, John (1631–1700). Poet, playwright, translator. *All for Love; Absalom and Achitophel; The Hind and the Panther; Alexander's Feast.*

Duffy, Maureen (b. 1933). Poet, playwright, novelist. *Memorials of the Quick & the Dead; Evesong.*

Eliot, George (1819–80). Novelist, critic, translator, poet. *The Spanish Gypsy; The Legend of Jubal, and Other Poems.*

Eliot, Thomas Stearns (1888–1965). Poet, playwright, critic, editor. *The Waste Land; Four Quartets; Murder in the Cathedral; The Family Reunion; Old Possum's Book of Practical Cats.*

Emerson, Ralph Waldo (1803–82). Essayist, poet. *The Problem; Each and All.*

Ewart, Gavin (b. 1916). Poet, editor, copywriter. *Londoners; Pleasures of the Flesh.*

Fuller, Roy (b. 1912). Poet, novelist, solicitor. *Brutus's Orchard; Tiny Tears.*

Gascoyne, David (b. 1916). Poet. *Elegiac Improvisation on the Death of Paul Eluard; The Sun at Midnight.*

Gay, John (1685–1732). Poet, playwright. *The Beggar's Opera; Acis and Galatea; Trivia.*

Gilbert, Sir William Schwenck (1836–1911). Poet, playwright, librettist. *Bab Ballads; The Palace of Truth.*

Goldsmith, Oliver (*c.* 1730–74). Poet, playwright, novelist, essayist. *The Deserted Village;* Song from *The Vicar of Wakefield* (novel).

Gordon, Adam Lindsay (1833–70). Poet, horseman. *The Sick Stockrider; How we Beat the Favourite.*

Gower, John (*c.* 1330–1408). Poet. *Speculum Meditantis; Vox Clamantis; Confessio Amantis.*

Gray, Thomas (1716–71). Poet, professor. *Elegy Written in a Country Churchyard; Ode on the Death of a Favourite Cat.*

Green, Matthew (1696–1737). Poet, customs official. *The Spleen; The Grotto.*

Hammerstein II, Oscar (1895–1960). Lyric writer. *Show Boat; Oklahoma; Carmen Jones.*

Hardy, Thomas (1840–1928). Novelist, short story writer, poet. *Wessex Poems; Satires of Circumstance; The Dynasts.*

Heine, Heinrich (1797–1856). Poet, prose writer. *Buch der Lieder.*

Herbert, George (1593–1633). Poet, clergyman. *The Temple.*

Herrick, Robert (1591–1674). Poet, clergyman, goldsmith. *To the Virgins, to Make Much of Time; Delight in Disorder.*

Hood, Thomas (1799–1845). Poet, editor. *Song of the Shirt; The Bridge of Sighs; Odes and Addresses to Great People.*

Hopkins, Gerard Manley (1844–89). Poet, Jesuit priest. *The Wreck of the Deutschland; Pied Beauty; The Windhover.*

Housman, Alfred Edward (1859–1936). Poet, classicist. *A Shropshire Lad; Last Poems.*

Hunt, Leigh (1784–1859). Editor, critic, poet. *Jenny Kissed Me; Abou ben Adhem.*

Johnson, Lionel Pigot (1867–1902). Poet, critic. *By the Statue of King Charles at Charing Cross; Oxford.*

Johnson, Samuel (1709–84). Lexicographer, editor, critic, poet. *The Vanity of Human Wishes; London.*

Jones, David (1895–1974). Poet, painter. *In Parenthesis; Anathemata.*

Jonson, Ben (1572–1637). Playwright, poet, masque writer. *Volpone; The Alchemist; To the Memory of My Beloved, the Author Mr William Shakespeare; An Ode: To Himself.*

Keats, John (1795–1821). Poet. *Endymion; Hyperion; The Eve of St Agnes; On a Grecian Urn; To Autumn; To a Nightingale.*

Kipling, Rudyard (1865–1936). Novelist, short story writer, journalist, poet. *Departmental Ditties; Barrack-Room Ballads.*

Kirkup, James (b. 1923). Poet, teacher. *The Body Servant; Heaven, Hell and Hari-Kari.*

Lamb, Charles (1775–1834). Essayist, poet, clerk. *The Old Familiar Faces; On an Infant Dying as Soon as Born.*

Landor, Walter Savage (1775–1864). Poet, prose writer. *Dirce; Rose Aylmer; Count Julian.*

Larkin, Philip (b. 1922). Poet, novelist, jazz critic, librarian. *High Windows; The Whitsun Weddings.*

Lawrence, David Herbert (1885–1930). Novelist, poet. *Birds, Beasts and Flowers; Pansies; Look. We Have Come Through!*

Lear, Edward (1812–88). Painter, poet. *Book of Nonsense; Nonsense Songs.*

Le Gallienne, Richard (1866–1947). Poet, essayist. *The Lonely Dancer.*

Longfellow, Henry Wadsworth (1807–82). Poet, linguist, translator. *The Song of Hiawatha; The Courtship of Miles Standish.*

Lovelace, Richard (1618–58). Soldier, poet. *To Althea; Lucasta; Epodes, Odes, Sonnets, Songs, etc.*

Lowell, James Russell (1819–91). Editor, poet. *A Fable for Critics.*

MacNeice, Louis (1907–63). Poet, radio script writer. *Autumn Journal; Autumn Sequel; Visitations.*

Marlowe, Christopher (1564–93). Playwright, poet. *Tamburlaine; Tragedy of Dr Faustus; Edward II; Come live with me and be my Love.*

Marston, John (*c.* 1575–1634). Playwright, poet. *The Metamorphosis of Pigmalion's Image and Certain Satyres.*

Marvell, Andrew (1621–78). Poet, politician. *The Garden; An Horatian Ode upon Cromwell's Return from Ireland; The Last Instructions to a Painter; To His Coy Mistress.*

Masefield, John (1878–1967). Poet, novelist, critic. *Sea Fever; Reynard the Fox; Cargoes.*

Meredith, George (1828–1909). Novelist, poet. *Modern Love; Phoebus with Admetus.*

Mew, Charlotte (1869–1928). Poet. *The Farmer's Bride; Fin de Fête; Ken.*

Milton, John (1608–74). Poet, pamphleteer, government official. *L'Allegro; Il Penseroso; Comus; Lycidas; Paradise Lost; Paradise Regained; Samson Agonistes; On His Blindness.*

Mitchell, Adrian (b. 1932). Poet, playwright, novelist. *Out Loud; Ride the Nightmare; To Whom It May Concern.*

Monro, Harold (1879–1932). Publisher, editor, bookseller, poet. *The Collected Poems of Harold Monro.*

Moore, Thomas (1779–1852). Poet, song writer. *Lalla Rookh; The Harp That Once through Tara's Halls.*

Morris, William (1834–96). Poet, designer, socialist. *The Earthly Paradise; The Defence of Guenevere.*

Muir, Edwin (1887–1959). Poet, novelist, critic, translator. *The Chorus of the Newly Dead; Variations on a Time Theme.*

Newman, John Henry (1801–90). Religious leader, teacher, writer. *Lead, Kindly Light; The Dream of Gerontius.*

Otway, Thomas (1652–85). Playwright, poet. *Venice Preserv'd.*

Patmore, Coventry (1823–96). Poet, museum official. *The Angel in the House; The Unknown Eros.*

Peacock, Thomas Love (1785–1866). Novelist, poet, official. *The Genius of the Thames; The Philosophy of Melancholy.*

Philips, Ambrose (*c.* 1675–1749). Poet. *To Miss Charlotte Pulteney in her Mother's arms.*

Philips, John (1676–1709). Poet. *Cyder.*

Plath, Sylvia (1932–63). Poet, novelist, short story writer. *The Colossus; Ariel; Winter Trees.*

Plomer, William (1903–73). Poet, novelist. *The Dorking Thigh; The Playboy of the Demi-World: 1938.*

Poe, Edgar Allan (1809–49). Poet, short story writer. *The Raven; Annabel Lee; The Bells.*

Pope, Alexander (1688–1744). Poet. *The Rape of the Lock; The Dunciad; An Essay on Man; Moral Essays.*

Pound, Ezra (1885–1972). Poet, critic. *Hugh Selwyn Mauberley; Cantos.*

Prior, Matthew (1664–1721). Diplomat, poet. *An English Padlock; A Better Answer.*

Quarles, Francis (1592–1644). Poet, courtier. *Emblems.*

Ralegh, Sir Walter (*c.* 1552–1618). Explorer, essayist, historian, poet. *Cynthia, the Lady of the Sea; The Lie; The Pilgrimage.*

Rimbaud, Arthur (1854–91). Poet, prose writer, traveller. *Le bateau ivre.*

Rochester, John Wilmot, 2nd Earl of (1647–80). Poet, wit. *A Satyr against Mankind; Upon Nothing; Maim'd Debauchee.*

Rogers, Samuel (1763–1855). Poet, banker. *The Pleasures of Memory.*

Ross, Alan (b. 1922). Poet, editor, cricket writer. *To Whom It May Concern.*

Rossetti, Christina (1830–94). Poet. *Goblin Market; Sing-Song; Monna Innominata.*

Rossetti, Dante Gabriel (1828–82). Poet, painter. *The House of Life; The Blessed Damozel; Jenny.*

Sackville, Charles, 6th Earl of Dorset (1638–1706). Courtier, poet. *To all you Ladies now at Land.*

Scott, Sir Walter (1771–1832). Novelist, poet, lawyer. *The Lay of the Last Minstrel; The Lady of the Lake; Marmion.*

Shadwell, Thomas (1642–92). Dramatist, poet. *The Medal of John Bayes; The Sullen Lovers.*

Shakespeare, William (1564–1616).)Playwright, poet. *Sonnets; Hamlet; Romeo and Juliet; As You Like It; Twelfth Night; King Lear; Richard II; A Midsummer Night's Dream.*

Shelley, Percy Bysshe (1792–1822). Poet. *Prometheus Unbound; Ode to the West Wind; To a Skylark; Adonais.*

Shirley, James (1596–1666). Poet, playwright, schoolmaster. *The Contention of Ajax and Ulysses.*

Sidney, Sir Philip (1554–86). Poet, statesman, soldier. *Astrophel and Stella; The Arcadia.*

Sitwell, Dame Edith (1887–1964). Poet, critic, biographer. *Façade; Still Falls the Rain; Elegy for Dylan Thomas.*

Smart, Christopher (1722–71). Poet, translator. *A Song to David; Jubilate Agno.*

Smith, Horace (1779–1849) and **James** (1775–1839). Novelist and solicitor respectively. *Rejected Addresses; Horace in London.*

Smith, Stevie (1902–71). Poet, novelist. *The Frog Prince; Scorpion; Not Waving but Drowning.*

Southey, Robert (1774–1843). Poet, biographer, historian. *The Battle of Blenheim; The Inchcape Rock; Madoc.*

Spark, Muriel (b. 1918). Novelist, short story writer, poet. *Collected Poems.*

Spender, Stephen (b. 1909). Poet, editor, critic. *The Landscape near an Aerodrome; Elegy for Margaret.*

Spenser, Edmund (*c.* 1552–99). Poet, official. *The Shepheards Calender; The Faerie Queene; Epithalamion.*

Swift, Jonathan (1667–1745). Satirist, pamphleteer, poet, dean. *Verses on his own Death; On Poetry, a Rhapsody; A Beautiful Young Nymph Going to Bed.*

Swinburne, Algernon Charles (1837–1909). Poet, critic, playwright. *Tristram of Lyonesse; Hymn to Proserpine; A Forsaken Garden.*

Tagore, Sir Rabindranath (1861–1941). Poet, novelist, teacher. *Gitanjali.*

Tate, Nahum (1652–1715). Poet, librettist. *Dido and Aeneas.*

Taylor, John (1580–1653). Waterman, poet. *All the Workes of John Taylor, the Water Poet.*

Tennyson, Alfred, 1st Baron (1809–92). Poet. *In Memoriam; A Dream of Fair Women; Morte d'Arthur; Locksley Hall; Maud; Idylls of the King.*

Thackeray, William Makepeace (1811–63). Novelist, essayist, ballad writer. *Sorrows of Werther; Little Billee.*

Thomas, Dylan (1914–53). Poet, prose writer. *Fern Hill; A Refusal to Mourn the Death, By Fire, of a Child in London; Poem in October; Do not go Gentle into that Good Night.*

Thompson, Francis (1859–1907). Poet, essayist. *The Hound of Heaven; Daisy.*

Thomson, James (1700–48). Poet, dramatist. *The Seasons; Liberty.*

Thwaite, Anthony (b. 1930). Poet, editor. *The Stones of Emptiness; A Portion for Foxes.*

Verlaine, Paul (1844–96). Poet. *Chanson d'automne; Soleils couchants.*

Webster, John (*c.* 1580–*c.* 1625). Playwright, poet. *The Duchess of Malfi; The White Devil; The Devil's Law-Case.*

Whitehead, William (1715–85). Poet, playwright. *The Sweepers; Variety, a Tale for Married People.*

Wilde, Oscar (1854–1900). Playwright, novelist, short story writer, poet. *The Ballad of Reading Gaol; Requiescat.*

Wolfe, Humbert (1886–1940). Poet, civil servant. *London Sonnets; Kensington Gardens in Wartime.*

Wordsworth, William (1770–1850). Poet. *The Prelude; Tintern Abbey; Intimations of Immortality; The Excursion; I Wandered Lonely as a Cloud; Composed upon Westminster Bridge.*

Wright, David (b. 1920). Poet, editor. *Adam at Evening; Nerve Ends.*

Wyatt, Sir Thomas (*c.* 1503–42). Diplomat, poet. *The Lover sheweth how he is forsaken of such as he sometime enjoyed; Comparison of love to a streame falling from the Alpes.*

Wycherley, William (*c.* 1640–1716). Playwright, poet. *Miscellany Poems.*

Yeats, William Butler (1865–1939). Poet, playwright. *The Rose; The Wild Swans at Coole; Michael Robartes and the Dancer; The Tower.*

Index